Jesus and Muhammad

2 Rays Of The Same Light

By

Karim Shabazz

This book is dedicated to the relativity and congruence found in the teachings of Jesus and Muhammad, and the wisdom this provides for all people of faith. May the critical insights in this book provoke thought, dispel ambiguity, and lend support to the world movement of interfaith and mutual relations.

Published by Bryteminds

ISBN 978-0-578-47366-6

Library of Congress Control Number: 2019907398

Contents

Preface...5

Introduction...8

Jesus and Muhammad: Clearing The Table,
Setting The Tone 11

2 Rays Of The Same Light: Why This Title? 13

Jesus and Muhammad: A Comparative Look At
Their Teaching 18

Jesus and Muhammad: Face-to-Face 20

Prayer 23

Judging Other People 29

True Righteousness versus Superficial Acts 31

Only G-d Is Holy And Perfectly Perfect 37

There Is But One G-d, Be Kind and Have Love
For Your Fellow Man 43

Remember G-d With Your Wealth and Material
Possessions 51

Contents

Jesus Taught Beatitudes on the Mountain Muhammad Taught Beatitudes on the Mountain...58

The Proof Is In The Pudding 69

Jesus and Muhammad: Prophets of The One G-d
....74

Jesus and Muhammad Advocated Active Participation From Their Followers 82

Jesus Promised The Coming of The Comforter.. 89

Muhammad: The Comforter, The Spirit of Truth
....104

The Quran: The Message Heard By Muhammad
....124

The Authenticity Of The Quran 128

The Quran Unveiled Mystery and Enhanced Science..131
The Seven Layers of the Sky and of the Earth .134

How Did Muhammad Know The Universe Was Expanding? 136

Contents

The Barrier Between Fresh Water and Salt Water..138

The Defeat and Victory of the Roman Empire 141

Jesus and Muhammad Practiced Fasting 145

Jesus & Muhammad Taught Principles of Interfaith..149

Epilogue 171

End Notes 178

Bibliography 208

Index 211

PREFACE

In the 58 years of my spectacular life, there are several things I have come to better understand and truly appreciate! For example, I have come to understand that everything in life has purpose and that nothing is coincidental. I have also come to understand that (1) historical events undoubtedly have a special significance, (2) historical events were predestined to occur, and (3) though miles away and many years apart, many historical figures often share a unique affiliation with each other. During my undergraduate studies at Clayton State University, my world history studies presented a plethora of chronicles that gave impetus to this outlook.

Always fascinated by science and intrigued by world history, as I actively participated in my history class and learned about significant events of the past, I began to realize that these events and the people involved were all part of a predetermined and well-orchestrated movement of social change, scientific-technological innovation, and spiritual awakening!

It dawned on me that, just as the arrangement of select stars in our skies form awe-struck constellations, quite visible on any clear night; I likewise deduced that key events and prominent individuals in history often form what I describe as "historical constellations". As such, there are several profound historical events and highly distinguished individuals who are "connected" by their mutual significance and social relevance. From this perspective, I reasoned that the key people in history were serving as "catalysts" and "precursors" to each other!

This observation is not merely my philosophical opinion, and surely not far-fetched. On the contrary, this idea of "relativity" is found in several empirical sciences such as biology, physiology, chemistry, and even geology, to name a few. During my postgraduate studies, I found this idea of "relativity" endorsed and cogently validated by the world-renowned physicist Albert Einstein, as it pertains to physics.

Various micro processes in biology, chemistry, botany, physics, genetics, and other observable sciences, provide numerous examples where something happens as a "precursor" to something else. These processes may be occurring in different places and at different times, but they are all part of and contribute to a specific and well calculated outcome.

As such, it should come as no surprise that just as in the sciences, certain historical events and especially the key people involved, also show evidence of "relativity". The more I studied and learned about some of the intriguing developments in world history, while paying close attention to the "unique characteristics" of the people involved; the more I saw these events and the people involved not as separate, unrelated incidents, but rather, as correlated and corresponding pieces belonging to the same progressive movement.

When carefully examined through unbiased lens, there are 2 highly significant people whose life, influence, and teaching, stand out as a profound religious and historical example of this relativity. As there is irrefutable evidence of relativity in the stars and empirical sciences, so it is in the humanities! It is with great pleasure and humble service that I present to you *JESUS AND MUHAMMAD, 2 RAYS OF THE SAME LIGHT!*   *Karim Shabazz*

Introduction

The purpose of this book is to share a compelling view of two highly significant people whose life, influence, and teaching, show remarkable examples of congruence, relativity, and complement. By no means were Jesus and Muhammad identical, but history and scriptures incessantly show diverse areas where their teaching, moral example, and ethical demeanor were quite similar, complementary, and historically relative to each other.

As a matter of fact, Jesus and Muhammad are more affiliated and historically relative than most people are aware of! Once again, they were not identical, but in this book the author intends to identify and carefully explore much of their significant relativity and congruence. The author humbly asks each reader to utilize two valuable assets in the pages to follow; they are the gifts of (1) **unbiased inductive observation** and (2) **sound deductive reasoning**. The author will also show how their "relativity" is not by coincidence or random serendipity; but by the plan of the All-Wise Creator, who gives purpose and significance to everything He decrees!

The author is very much aware of the skeptics, as well as the wide spread misinformation and misconceptions that exist regarding a comparative look at Jesus and Muhammad. The internet and publication market are full of "biased comparisons" that tend to misconstrue and over-exaggerate their "negligible differences", but they often fail to adequately identify and highlight the grander scale and bigger picture; their likeness, relativity, and congruence!

Some authors and historians who do acknowledge some of their likeness and similarities, tend to briefly mention and underscore them; preferring to over-exaggerate those trivial features where they were obviously unlike. It is their unique commonalities however, that contain much more intrigue, intellectual merit for constructive discussion, and far greater utility for building bridges of peace and friendship. If one were to examine their moral example and especially the letter and spirit of their teaching, they would see that **Jesus** and **Muhammad** are like *2 RAYS OF THE SAME LIGHT*.

In preparation for this book, the author has done extensive research of various sources, particularly the Bible and the Quran, in hopes of presenting an unbiased and circumspect picture. The author is aware that many people of faith who identify with Christianity, Islam, and Judaism, may already have "set views" of Jesus and Muhammad. Many of these views, albeit sincere, could possibly benefit from an "unbiased second look".

Whether abroad in the Middle East or here in the United States, we all share the same space and breathe the same air. We all have the same basic needs, concerns, fears, and interests. If there was ever a time to better understand each other and build upon our commonalities for mutual respect and global peace; that time would be now!

The hope of this book is to shed light upon a subject overwhelmingly obscured by misconceptions and wide spread misinformation. With clarity, perhaps the followers of Jesus and Muhammad can become closer friends of faith, respecting each other's autonomy; while working together to make the world a better place to live and co-exist in peace and understanding.

JESUS AND MUHAMMAD

Clearing The Table, Setting The Tone

Before making our swan dive into the exegesis of this book, the author deems it necessary to "clear the table", as well as "set the tone." As you proceed through this book, you will notice that each time when referring to The Creator, the word "The" and "Creator" always begin with capital letters. This is because the author considers the majesty of G-d to be deserving of such lofty distinction and honorable recognition at every mentioning. You will also notice throughout this book that the spelling "G o d", is never used when referring to The Creator, instead you will find that the spelling "G-d" is used as a substitute. The author takes the position that because the spelling of the English word "god", when reversed, unfortunately spells the word "dog", that such is not befitting as an honorable reference for The Creator.[1] While this may be trivial or having no intended pun to the novice reader, suffice it to say, the author considers the noble and exalted status of The Creator to be deserving of the highest reverence and sacred respect. This attitude is validated by the prayer taught by Jesus in Matthew of the New Testament, "Our Father in heaven, hallowed be your name." Therefore, the name that references The Lord is to always be "hallowed," and hallowed means holy, sacred, blessed, greatly revered and respected. Hence, G-d is used, and not G o d, when referring to The Lord.

Also, it is to be understood that whenever the name Jesus or Muhammad is mentioned anywhere throughout this book, the salutations of "peace and blessings be upon him", should be honorably acknowledged. The author is regardful of the prominent significance of Jesus and Muhammad and wishes that each reader be mindful of the honorable salutation that they are both due, whenever their name is mentioned.[2]

Jesus and Muhammad

2 Rays Of The Same Light: Why This Title?

Unarguably, the sun emits powerful rays that are vitally important and essential to our physical existence. Some rays of the sun give us bright light, which dispels the darkness of night and enables us to see clearly during the day. Other powerful rays of the sun provide the earth with heat, which protects us from feeling cold. These 2 types of rays emitted from the sun are not only significant and necessary for our physical existence, they are also representative and symbolic of two much needed essentials for our social existence![1]

Heat is symbolic and representative of our *"moral intelligence"* and *"moral sensitivity"*, the way we *should* "naturally think, naturally feel, and naturally respond" to matters of concern. As the absence or lack of physical heat leaves us eventually feeling physically cold; like-wise, the absence or lack of *"moral intelligence and moral sensitivity"* makes us eventually become "cold hearted", "uncaring", and "insensitive" to the natural and civic rights of others.[2]

Light is also symbolic and representative of our *"spiritual awareness"* and *"spiritual intelligence"*, how we *should* "naturally consider, honor, and regard" our Creator. People who have a sincere belief in and mindful regard for the Creator, naturally have a spiritual awareness and spiritual intelligence about them. This spiritual component is a "force" that other people can feel from their presence, as well as a "light" that they can see emanating through their personality and character! [3]

The author has presented *Jesus and Muhammad as 2 Rays of The Same Light,* to highlight the complementary likeness of their *moral intelligence* and *spiritual awareness.* The *moral intelligence* taught and excellently demonstrated by Jesus, was in turn exemplified and corroborated by the *moral intelligence* in Muhammad.

Similarly, the *spiritual awareness* distinctly observed in Muhammad, was superbly and without question, epitomized and demonstrated by the spiritual awareness of Jesus. Their teaching, moral example, and ethical demeanor were designed to reinstate man's moral intelligence and spiritual awareness; without which, man is essentially no more noble than the animals. [4]

Moral intelligence and spiritual awareness are perhaps the two most essential qualities man must possess, if there is to ever be any resemblance of heaven here on earth. Human life is comprised of diverse interests and pursuits such as politics, education, culture, and religion, to name a few. Other interests such as science and technology, commerce, public health, civic laws governing what is lawful and unlawful, race and ethnic diversity, etc., are all significant and equally important.

If man is to ever co-exist in peace and mutual good will with his fellow-man in a diverse world such as ours, he must have moral sensitivity and spiritual awareness.

Commentary [handwritten annotation]

The teaching of Jesus and Muhammad, though comprised of various subject matters addressing diverse issues, each have two common threads embedded throughout their entire message; those two threads are moral intelligence and spiritual consciousness!

The pages ahead will show a striking resemblance and likeness in the moral intelligence and spiritual awareness of Jesus and Muhammad; as evidenced by their teaching and practical example. The author contends that this "likeness" is not by coincidence, on the contrary, it is because **Jesus and Muhammad are 2 Rays of the Same Light!**   *3rd person* [handwritten annotation]

If, as the author contends, **Jesus and Muhammad are 2 Rays of the Same Light**; it then becomes incumbent upon all who "claim" to follow Jesus and all who "claim" to follow Muhammad, to change their previous attitudes and perceptions of each other. This is common sense that, unfortunately, is not too common!

This "common sense", requires us to recognize our valuable commonalities and similar inherent values, as evidenced from the similar values and principles in the teachings of Jesus and Muhammad; and begin to see each other as friends of faith and supporters of each other's good works.

As presented from the Bible (Matthew 6: 9-10 New International version), Jesus taught his followers to pray, "Our Father in heaven, hallowed be Your Name, Your Kingdom come, Your Will be done, on earth as it is in heaven". Muhammad taught, as presented in the Quran (chapter 13 verse 11), "Verily G-d does not change the condition of any people, until they first change that which is within themselves".

In comparison, Jesus taught people to recognize G-d as being hallowed (highly revered, respected, and honored), and to pray that <u>His</u> Kingdom come, and <u>His</u> Will be done on earth (in our schools, government, neighborhoods, home, etc.), as it is in heaven. Muhammad taught and reminded people that, if you want heaven to be here on earth, you must first change what is within yourself, to conform to what is acceptable in G-d's kingdom and pleasing to His will!

There is a dual significance and relationship in the words spoken by Jesus and Muhammad. On the one hand as Jesus taught, we must sincerely pray to G-d with reverence and honor, asking that His Kingdom come and that His Will be done on earth like it is in heaven. Yes, we must sincerely pray for this day and night!

In addition to this as Muhammad taught, as we turn to G-d humbly in prayer, asking that His Kingdom and Will be done here on earth like it is in heaven; we must first be the change that we want to see throughout the earth! By first changing that which is within our own selves (our attitudes, our moral and spiritual values), we in turn establish a heaven-like state of being within our own self, thereby maximizing the synergies between the power of prayer and individual action!

The words from the Quran that Muhammad spoke, "verily G-d does not change the condition of any people, until they first change that which is within themselves";

is virtually synonymous with another concept Jesus taught, found in Luke 17: 20-21 of the Bible,

> "And when he (Jesus) was demanded of the Pharisees, when the kingdom of G-d should come, he answered them and said, The kingdom of G-d comes not with observation: neither shall they say, Lo here! or Lo there! For, behold, the kingdom of G-d is within you".

Jesus clearly states that the "kingdom of G-d" is not located at a physical location here or there, but that it is within you! In congruence, Muhammad clearly states that G-d will not change the condition of any people, until they first change that which is within themselves! Jesus and Muhammad teachings are obviously emanating from the same perspective, clearly addressing the same central idea, simply put, cut from the same cloth.[5]

Jesus and Muhammad

A Comparative Look At Their Teaching

To adequately identify and explore the commonalities that exist in the teachings of Jesus and Muhammad, we must shrewdly examine the Bible and the Quran. The Bible, more specifically the New Testament, is the definitive source to adequately explore the message and teaching of Jesus; and the Quran is the definitive source to sufficiently explore the message and teaching of Muhammad. The last major speech of Muhammad, historically referred to as "The Farewell Address", is an additional reference we will explore later. We will simultaneously examine and compare this major address of Muhammad to the well-known address of Jesus, often referred to as "The Sermon On The Mount", and "The Beatitudes", as we continue to highlight commonalities in their message.

There are also reported sayings of Muhammad referred to as "hadith" that can also serve as an additional reference, however the Quran will be our primary reference, and in fact, the definitive source for our discussion here.[1] As we examine their teaching as found in select passages of the Bible and Quran, it is essential to consider some of the prominent issues and social matters of concern that both Jesus and Muhammad were surrounded by, confronted with, and found it necessary to address.

Though approximately 769 miles away and nearly 570 years apart from each other, Jesus and Muhammad, as evidenced by the critical similarities in their teaching, were obviously closer in mind and spirit than most people know. Despite the abundance of misinformation and divisive propaganda that often seeks to present Jesus and Muhammad as estranged opponents, the author is confident that the comparative review and critical insights presented in this book, is adequate food for thought for anyone who wishes to think outside of the box!

Karim Shabazz

Jesus and Muhammad: Face to Face

*I*n presenting Jesus and Muhammad face-to-face, the author has decided to present a side by side comparative look at select verses from the New Testament taught by Jesus and select verses from the Quran taught by Muhammad. By doing so, each reader can see the familiar topic being addressed, the words being spoken, and the similar context in which they were conveyed.

Please note, the author is conducting this comparative review upon the premise, that each reader is aware that the teachings of Jesus were not actually from himself, or self-inspired; they were, as he himself described in John 17:6,

"My teaching is not my own, it comes from the One who sent me".[1]

Likewise, the reader should understand, the teachings of the Quran that Muhammad taught were not from himself either or self-inspired, but they too, are from the same One who gave Jesus his teaching; The All-Knowing, Most Gracious, Creator of the heavens and the earth.

Identifying the origin and purpose of the Quran, G-d says in the Quran, chapter 3:1-3

"Allah(G-d)! There is no one worthy of worship but He, The Living, The Self-Subsisting, Eternal. It is He who sent down to you (Muhammad) the Book in truth, confirming what went before it: and He sent down the Law (of Moses) and the Gospel (of Jesus) before this, as a guide for mankind, and He sent down the criterion (of judgement between right and wrong").[2]

20

The author has mentioned this for two specific reasons. (1) Due to many years of promotional religious broadcast, media, and favorable historic mention, most people, especially in the United States, give automatic credibility and authentic regard to the mention of Jesus and the New Testament. (2) On the contrary, due to many years of tainted journalism, misinformation, skepticism of the unknown, and biased historical mention; many people, especially in the United States, are hesitant and doubtful of the credibility and authenticity of Muhammad and the Quran.

In addition to this, there is the all-too-often negative media coverage, fear, and stereotyping of Islam and Muslims, now labeled as "Islamophobia", due to several terrorist attacks committed by persons who call themselves Muslims. These terrorist activities have been wrongfully associated with Islam, Muhammad, and the Quran.[3]

Even though these terrorist activities have been and still are, vehemently condemned and publicly denounced by sincere and faithful Muslims all around the world, there remains a heavily distorted and negative image of Islam: which indirectly gets associated with Muhammad and the Quran.

The author therefore wishes to appeal to each readers' higher reasoning and rational faculties: to not judge Islam, Muhammad, and the Quran by the actions of people who *call themselves Muslims*; but rather, judge the people who *call themselves Muslims*, by the Quran and the true ethical manner in which Muhammad actually lived.[4] In like manner, we should not judge Christianity or Judaism, by the actions of people *who call themselves Christians and Jews*; but rather, we should judge the people who *call themselves Christians and Jews*, by the excellent character and manner in which Jesus and Moses actually lived.[5]

By this standard, each reader is encouraged to be open-minded, unbiased, and equitable, as they learn of the commonalities in Jesus and Muhammad's teaching. Let us now identify and explore some of their likeness and unique similarities!

P R A Y E R

One of the first similarities the author found note-worthy about Jesus and Muhammad was their devout attitude regarding prayer and what was expressed in their prayer.[1] What a person says while praying to G-d indicates much about their level of devotion, humility, and spiritual attention. A comparative look at what Jesus and Muhammad expressed in their prayers, shows a remarkable resemblance of their humility, devotion, and mindfulness of their need and dependency on G-d. It also shows their recognition that it is G-d alone who grants pardon, forgiveness, and guidance; and that He is The One deserving the praise and reverence!

According to Matthew 6: 5-13 of the New Testament, Jesus said,

"And when you pray, you must not be like the hypocrites. For they love to stand and pray in the synagogues and at the street corners, that they may be seen by others. Truly I say unto you; they have received their reward. But when you pray, go into your room and shut the door and pray to your Father who is in secret, and your Father who sees in secret will reward you. And when you pray, do not heap up empty phrases as the Gentiles do, for they think that they will be heard for their many words. Do not be like them, for your Father knows what you need before you ask him. Pray then like this: (1) "Our Father in heaven, hallowed be Your name. (2) Your kingdom come, Your will be done, (3) on earth as it is in heaven. (4) Give us this day, our daily bread, (5) and forgive us our debts, as we also have forgiven our debtors. (6) And lead us not into temptation, but deliver us from evil. (7) For Yours is the kingdom, and the power, and the glory, forever. Amen." [2]

Interestingly, a prayer that Muhammad often prayed and which happens to be the first chapter of the

Quran, is called *"The Al Fatiha"*, which means "The Opening". It is as follows,

(1) "In the name of Allah (G-d), The Most Gracious, The Most Merciful; (2) all praise is due to Allah (G-d), the Cherisher and Sustainer of all the worlds; (3) The Most Gracious, The Most Merciful; (4) Master of the Day of Judgement; (5) You do we worship and Your aid do we seek;(6) Guide us on the Straight Way; (7) The Way of those on whom You have bestowed Your Grace, not the way of those who incur Your displeasure and wrath; nor the way of those who have gone astray. Ameen.[3]

Let us now identify the stated and inferred similarities

(1) Both Jesus and Muhammad's prayer begin by giving devout acknowledgement of G-d and reverence to His name.

Jesus begins: "Our Father in heaven, hallowed (holy and blessed) be Your name".

Muhammad begins: "In the name of Allah (G-d), The Most Gracious, The Most Merciful; all praise is due to Allah (G-d), the Lord of all the worlds; The Most Gracious, The Most Merciful; Master of the Day of Judgement".

(2) Both Jesus and Muhammad proceed in expressing humble devotion to G-d, but now in the second person singular!

Jesus continues: "YOUR kingdom come, YOUR will be done, on earth like it is in heaven".

Muhammad continues: "YOU do we worship, and YOUR aid do we seek".

(3) Both Jesus and Muhammad continue by now <u>asking</u> for something specific!

Jesus continues: "Give us this day, our daily bread; and forgive us our trespasses (sins), as we forgive those who trespass (sin) against us".

Muhammad continues: "Guide us on the Straight Way, The Way of those on whom You have bestowed Your Grace".

(4) Both Jesus and Muhammad begin closure by asking G-d to protect them from sin and the subtle vices in society.

Jesus starts closure: "And lead us not into temptation, but deliver us from evil; for Yours is the Kingdom, and the Power, and the Glory, forever".

Muhammad starts closure: "Not the way of those who incur YOUR displeasure and wrath, nor the way of those who have gone astray".

(5) Both Jesus and Muhammad close with one word which means let it be.

Jesus says: "Amen"

Muhammad also said: "Ameen"

It is interesting that both the prayer of Jesus and the prayer of Muhammad immediately begin with devout acknowledgement of G-d and reverence for His name, both proceed to address G-d in the second person singular, both humbly ask G-d for something specific, both ask G-d to protect us from sin and the subtle vices in society, and both close with (let it be) Amen/Ameen, and last but surely not least, both are composed of seven verses.

The author contends that the profound similarities noted in Jesus and Muhammad's prayer are (1) clear, (2) mutually compatible and consistent with each other, and (3) illustrate too much resemblance to be by mere chance or random coincidence!

Another similarity in Jesus and Muhammad on the topic of prayer, is that they both issue the same caution not to pray as a hypocrite! In Matthew chapter 6, beginning at verse 5, Jesus says,

"And when you pray, you must not be like the hypocrites. For they love to stand and pray in the synagogues and at the street corners, that they may be seen by others".

Not surprisingly, Muhammad admonished this same caution that Jesus did, as mentioned in the Quran chapter 107, beginning with verse 4, where it says,

"So woe to the worshippers who are neglectful of their prayers, those who only want to be seen by other people, but refuse to give neighborly needs".

Therefore, not only is the prayer of Jesus and Muhammad in sync and consistent with each other, the fact that they both issue the same caution of "avoiding the character of the hypocrites who pray publicly to be seen by others", further demonstrates their likeness of mind and spirit in admonishing their people to be true and sincere, not superficial and pretentious!

In addition, not only is the prayer of Jesus and the prayer of Muhammad complementary to each other, it is also reported that Jesus and Muhammad prayed in similar fashion. It is documented in the New Testament that Jesus fell to his face to pray to G-d. Matthew 26:39 reads as follows...

"And going a little further, he (Jesus) fell on his face and prayed..."

In summary, Jesus and Muhammad both humbly prostrated in prayer to G-d, The One and Only, Maker of heaven and earth, who is Most Gracious and Most Merciful; they both expressed reverence for His name; both expressed their desire to be guided right by G-d, and the need of His help to avoid temptation and the subtle influences of the world that lead one to evil and going astray. Jesus and Muhammad, similar prayers, likeness of mind, spirit, and expression. Let the temples, churches, and mosques say Amen!

The author asks each reader to do the math: If two people, one speaking Aramaic and the other speaking Arabic, pray to the same One G-d, the Creator of heaven and earth, using similar words, similar expressions, similar format and context, making similar requests, in similar grammatical composition, both asking G-d to guide them and protect them from the temptations and evil influences in society, both mentioning reverence for His name, one asking G-d's Kingdom and Will to be done on earth like it is in heaven, the other stating that it is G-d only who deserves worship and His help is what we need, and both conclude with Amen; are they not in agreement and on one accord?

Judging Other People

According to Matthew 7: 1-5, Jesus said,

"Judge not, that you be not judged. For with the judgement you pronounce, you will be judged, and with the measure you use, it will be measured to you. Why do you see the speck that is in your brother's eye, but do not notice the log that is in your own eye? Or how can you say to your brother, let me take the speck out of your eye; when there is a log in your own eye? You hypocrite, first take the log out of your own eye, and then you will see clearly to take the speck out of your brother's eye".

Muhammad taught the same principle in similar words, for it is written in the Quran 2: 44-46,

"Do you enjoin right conduct on other people, and forget to practice it yourselves, and yet you study the same scripture? Will you not understand? Nay, seek Allah's help with patient perseverance and prayer: it is indeed hard, except to those who bring a humble spirit; who bear in mind the certainty that they are going to meet their Lord, and that they are to return to Him".

REFLECTION

Jesus and Muhammad address this tendency many people of faith have, this tendency of "judging other people" while they themselves have the same or similar faults, sometimes even more.[1] Jesus identifies this habit in the people and boldly refers to those who do this as "You hypocrite"! The author considers it safe to say that, if Jesus wanted to address this subject more delicately or with softer admonishment, he certainly could have done so. On the contrary, he vehemently addressed this and identified those who do this as "hypocrite"! He directs the individual to FIRST remove the "log" from their own eye, so they can see clearly the speck in their brother's eye. Obviously a "log" is much larger than a "speck", this comparison therefore implies that the "fault-finder" typically has much more about their own self that needs to be improved upon and corrected, than the trivial and insignificant matter concerning the other person.

Muhammad also addressed this tendency in people of faith. The Quran is explicit in saying, "do you enjoin right conduct on the people, but forget to practice it yourself?"

Like Jesus, Muhammad saw people professing to be upright and righteous, but who were "fixated" on fault-finding and judging others whom they considered not as "holy" as them; but in truth, they themselves were not walking on the straight and narrow.

COMPARATIVE REVIEW

The teaching of Jesus and the teaching of Muhammad are once again congruent and on the same accord. Both address this hypocritical tendency of "fault-finding" and "judging" others we consider not as "righteous" as ourselves; while we have faults of our own, maybe even more. The fact that each of them addressed this issue, indicates that they both understood and valued the importance of "self-accountability," versus finding shortcomings and faults in other people. Jesus called those who do this, "hypocrites", and Muhammad equally reminded that we should have a humble spirit and remember that we all must return to G-d for judgement.

TRUE RIGHTEOUSNESS VERSUS SUPERFICIAL ACTS

According to Matthew, 7: 21-23, Jesus taught;

"Not everyone who says to me Lord, Lord; will enter the kingdom of heaven, but the one who does the will of my Father in heaven. On that day many will say to me, "Lord, Lord, did we not prophecy in your name, and cast out demons in your name, and do many mighty works in your name?' And then will I declare to them, "I never knew you, depart from me, you workers of lawlessness".[1]

According to the Quran, 2: 177, Muhammad taught;

"It is not righteousness that you turn your faces towards East or West; but it is righteousness to believe in Allah(G-d) and the Last Day, and the Angels, and the Book, and the Messengers, and to spend out of your substance and out of love for Him(G-d), for your kin, for the orphans, for the needy, for the wayfarer, for those who ask, and for the ransom of slaves; to be steadfast in prayer, and practice regular charity; to fulfill the contracts which you have made, and to be firm and patient in pain or suffering and adversity; and throughout all periods of panic. Such are the people of truth, the G-d-fearing".[2]

REFLECTION

Jesus and Muhammad now address a subject of vast applicability. The author considers this perhaps the "meat-and-potatoes" aspect of understanding the authentic message of Jesus and Muhammad. They both identify the difference between true righteousness versus what the author calls "superficial gestures and actions done for public display".

Jesus goes right to the point and identifies what may be described as "superficial gestures" and

31

"pretentious actions" supposedly done in "his name"; however, he abruptly states that this is not the will of G-d!

Jesus leaves no room for speculation; he explicitly said that not everyone who says "Lord, Lord" will enter the kingdom of heaven; he further states that there will be many who will say to him, "Lord, Lord, did we not prophecy in "Your name", and cast out demons in "Your name", and do many mighty works in "Your name"?; at which time he would say, "I never knew you, depart from me, you workers of lawlessness". It is almost as if Jesus envisioned the future and could see many who would be claiming his name, but not actually DOING THE WILL OF G-d! Having said these things with truth and candor, Jesus has their bases (senses) loaded!

Then we have Muhammad up to bat (figuratively speaking), who truly hits a home run by echoing the same point that Jesus did, but with more detailed description about the measure of righteousness and what is the "will of G-d". According to the words of Jesus, the people doing all those things supposedly in "his name" were not doing the true "will of G-d", he referred to them as "workers of lawlessness". Lawlessness implies the absence of law, and law is synonymous with rules and standards.

The author contends that the message of the Quran revealed to Muhammad was a "graceful" reminder of the excellent principles Jesus taught on righteousness. Interestingly, as in the message of Jesus, the Quran starts off by stating what righteousness is not.[3]

It starts by stating "It is not righteousness that you turn your faces towards East or West". This verse explicitly pertained to the followers of Muhammad who were meticulous and highly conscientious of which direction to turn towards for salat (prayer). However, the act of being meticulous and highly conscientious of facing the proper direction of prayer was not to be considered a proof or measurement of how pious and righteous they were! Too often, man starts to devote so much zealous attention and "over emphasis" to a ritual and custom, that he loses sight of the underlying moral and lesson that the ritual is pointing to.[4]

The Quran goes on to state that it is righteousness to first believe in G-d and the Last Day, and the Book, and the Messengers, to spend of your substance out of love for Him(G-d), for your kin(relatives), for orphans, for the needy, for the wayfarer, for those who ask, and for the ransom of slaves; to be steadfast in prayer and practice regular charity; to fulfill the contracts which you have made, and to be firm and patient in pain, suffering, and adversity; and throughout all periods of panic: such are the people of truth, the G-d-fearing!

These precepts that Muhammad taught from the Quran measure righteousness in the abstract context, as well as in our actions and deeds that affect change in society. By first addressing belief in G-d and belief in the Last Day, man is reminded that faith in G-d is number one, the top priority; and then one must believe in the Last Day, that is, the Day of Judgement when all must return to G-d for determination of our fate for heaven or hell, reward or punishment.

Included in the measure of righteousness concerning the abstract, is (1) having a belief in the angels (which are select agents and automated mediums G-d uses to carry out specific tasks), (2) having a belief in the Book (which refers to all the messages of revelation G-d has revealed), (3) having a belief in the Messengers (which is inclusive of all the prophets and messengers detailed by G-d over time). After identifying righteousness on the level of abstract and theoretical beliefs, G-d describes righteousness in terms of how we are to be considerate of others and spend a portion of our material wealth to (1) assist our kin(family and relatives), (2) the orphans, (3) for the needy (which could be anyone who needs and we are in a position to help), (4) for the wayfarer (who is also someone needy, except this is someone in need whom you come across while in route of your travels), (5) for those who ask (which is someone asking for a smaller favor, perhaps not as urgent as the needy), (6) and for the ransom of slaves; obviously, this item requires extended discussion.

The mention of "for the ransom of slaves" tells us that G-d wants those people asserting to be "believers" and "doers of His Will", to be concerned about and willing to sacrifice for the freedom and liberty of those who are slaves.[5] To sacrifice a portion of your resources to help free a slave demonstrates a high degree of humanitarian concern and character, and that is why it was included as one of the benchmarks of righteousness in the Quran. The author considers the mentioning of spending for "the ransom of slaves" to not only refer to those held captive in physical slavery. The connotative meaning is to also be concerned for the "freedom and liberation" of those held in mental and spiritual captivity and oppression. In the New Testament, Matthew 5:3, Jesus said "Blessed are the poor in spirit, for theirs is the kingdom of heaven". Being poor in spirit, is virtually consistent with those who are spiritually depressed, economically destitute, socially impoverished, academically despondent, and therefore held back from the higher pursuit of liberty and true happiness!

This mentioning in the Quran of spending for "the ransom of slaves" that Muhammad taught, is therefore consistent with the "Beatitude" of what Jesus taught about those poor in spirit!

The verse from the Quran continues along the theme of righteousness with being steadfast in prayer and regular in charity. To be steadfast in prayer and regular in charity indicates that a person prays often and regularly, not occasionally or only when in trouble or despair; and that they are mindful of the obligation to sacrifice from some of what G-d has blessed them with, to contribute to the well-being of others.

The verse continues by telling us to "fulfill the contracts which we have made". G-d knows that if there is to be any sense of trust domestically and internationally, man must be willing to honor the contracts and agreements he has made with others. As such, G-d gives the reminder here that a part of how "righteous" we are is measured by how well we keep our promises and commitments.

This verse on righteousness concludes by mentioning that a part of righteousness is "being resolute and patient even in pain, suffering, and adversity; and throughout periods of alarm and panic; that such are the people of truth, the G-d-fearing"! This is important because in times of pain, suffering, adversity, and especially alarm and panic; it is easy to feel despair and lamentation. The chapter in the Bible called "Lamentations" is a good example of this. Sometimes we all will experience some degree of suffering and adversity, as well as alarm and panic. It may be because of our own disobedience and transgression, as in Lamentations of the Bible; or it may be simply because G-d is conditioning your muscles of patience and testing your ability to endure without losing faith.

In summation, Jesus and Muhammad both expressed what righteousness is not, and they both identified righteousness as actually doing the "will of G-d". The message of Muhammad from the Quran shakes hands with the message of Jesus in the New Testament. Both teaching aim at making the believer more a person of upright and constructive action, and less a person of "lip professing". If more of the followers of Jesus and Muhammad did better at following these truths, it would positively influence the lives and well- being of society. There would be much more "actually doing", of the righteous things Jesus and Muhammad advocated, and much less lip service and pointing the finger at others.

Jesus and Muhammad: Only G-d Is Holy and Perfectly Perfect

The author considers this next discussion one that is likely to provoke some difference of opinion and perhaps some heated discussion. The author is aware of the strong sentimental attachment and extremely high estimation faithful followers have of Jesus and Muhammad. For many devout Christians and Muslims, Jesus and Muhammad are not only held in extremely high estimation with passionate attachment, they are sometimes mistakenly viewed as "holy, divine, or perfectly perfect". While Jesus and Muhammad were both exemplary models of having "perfect intentions", that is, they both epitomized the example of what G-d expects from every individual (having nothing but good, respectful, and honorable intentions); it is to be understood however that only G-d is truly "Perfectly Perfect". G-d alone is The Only One that is Free of all needs, requires nothing at all from the creation He made for His subsistence, not subject to sleep, fatigue, or slumber, never thirsts or hungers, knows all things and has such power that never dwindles or diminishes; Perfectly Perfect, Complete, and Unique!

Jesus himself is on record for teaching this, as it is noted in the New Testament Luke 18: verses 18-22,

And a certain ruler asked him, saying, "Good Master, what shall I do to inherit eternal life?" And Jesus said to him, "Why do you call me good? No one is good except G-d alone. You know the commandments: Do not commit adultery, Do not murder, Do not steal, Do not bear false witness, Honor your father and mother". And he (the ruler) said, All these I have kept since my youth". When Jesus heard this, he said to him, "One thing you still lack. Sell all that you have and distribute it to the poor, and you will have treasure in heaven; and come follow me." [1]

Muhammad taught the same, in words similar, as found in the Quran, chapter 18 verse 110:

Say: "I am but a man like you, but the inspiration has come to me, that your G-d is One G-d; and whoever expects to meet his Lord, let him work righteousness, and in the worship of his Lord, admit no one as partner". [2]

REFLECTION

In the scenario of Jesus, chapter 18 of Luke verse 18, Jesus was addressed as "Good Master", and much to the surprise of the person addressing Jesus, his response was, "Why do you call me good? No one is good except G-d alone"!

The author contends that for Jesus to reply the way he did, tells us that some people had already began to "adore" and "revere" him as holy, perfect, and deserving of such high praise and glory. His reply however, makes a bold, clear cut distinction between himself and G-d! Being referred to as "Good Master" or "Good Teacher", it is to be understood that the word "Good" in this context, implies such attributes as perfect, holy, and deserving of high praise and glory. Jesus replied, "No one is good except G-d". This means he wanted the people to understand that only G-d is "good" in the context of being Holy, Perfect, and deserving of praise, glory and worship; and he clearly did not want people to perceive him as such!

He wanted people to have sincere faith in G-d, to believe in the "good news" he had been given to teach, and more importantly, he wanted people to recognize the importance of "doing the will of G-d". He wanted people to understand that the power he possessed to do certain miracles came from G-d, and not himself. As previously mentioned, he also stated and wanted people to understand that his teaching was not from "himself", but that it was from G-d.

So in essence Jesus was saying, "Do not revere and adore me as the one to be praised and worshipped for my teaching, my power to do various miracles, my wisdom, and all these honorable accolades you're giving me; don't do it, because all these gifts and powers are from G-d, not me, and only He is deserving and worthy of such praise and worship; whatever "goodness" you see in me, is because I am doing the will of G-d, and He is the real Good Master." This is the essence of Jesus saying, "Why do you call me "Good Master? No one is good except G-d alone!

In the words from the Quran chapter 18 verse 110, taught by Muhammad, we find essentially the same message. Similar to Jesus, Muhammad expressed these words at a time when some people started to perceive him as divine, holy, and/or perfect, and just as Jesus was directed to say what he said, Muhammad was directed to say "I am but a mortal like you, but the inspiration has come to me, that your G-d is One G-d; and whoever expects to meet his Lord, let him work righteousness, and in the worship of his Lord, admit no one as an associate or partner".

Once again, the teaching of Muhammad shows congruence and resemblance to the message of Jesus. As Jesus shrewdly disapproved of being called "Good Master", but instead taught that no one is good except G-d alone; Muhammad said, "I am but a mortal human being like you". These two statements from Jesus and Muhammad are pointing to the same moral and logic.

If no one is "good" (divine, perfectly perfect, holy, deserving glory and worship) except G-d alone, as Jesus said, then Jesus was implying that, though he possessed profound wisdom, and could perform many undeniable miracles, was born immaculately by the will and power of G-d and chosen by G-d to guide people to truth and righteousness; yet despite all this, he too was a human person like everyone else who need G-d's Help! He repeatedly demonstrated that he was a mortal human being needing strength, direction, inspiration and G-d's help, by withdrawing from his disciples and crowds of people on several occasions, so that he could turn to G-d in prayer and solitude! Think about it...If Jesus wasn't in need of something, needing some degree of help, strength, inspiration, or re-fueling, why did he have to stop, depart from his disciples, and turn to G-d in prayer as often as he did? [3]

That's exactly what we as mortal human beings do, we turn to "The One" who is not mortal! We turn to G-d who is Holy, Perfectly Perfect, Divine, having All Power and such Power that never weakens or diminishes, Knowing All Things, Who Never Sleeps or Slumbers, Who Created all that exists, but Who Himself was never Created or Made, Who is Most Gracious, Most Merciful, All

Hearing and All Seeing, and Who answers the prayers of those who turn to Him in devotion!

Muhammad shared a similar situation and experience as Jesus did, not identical, but indeed similar. Jesus was inspired with the "Good News", commonly referred to as "The Gospel", by way of the Holy Spirit. Muhammad was also inspired by the Holy Spirit, with what is known as "AL Quran", which is Arabic for "The Book to be recited and proclaimed". The author is aware that some people, after reading that "Muhammad was also inspired by the Holy Spirit with the Quran", perhaps have a much different perspective about "The Quran" and its origin.

In anticipation of those who are not familiar with the Quran, its contents and origin, and who perhaps have some reservations or well intended doubts, as well as for those who may consider themselves already informed and have their views and perspectives already set; the author has reserved another section of this book that provides "clear and undebatable proof" of the Qurans' authenticity, origin, and validity, that each reader should enjoy contemplating.

None the less, suffice it to say both Jesus and Muhammad vehemently renounced and personally rejected the idea of themselves being considered perfect, holy, or worthy of worship; instead, they attributed these characteristics and qualities only to G-d! The fact that Jesus teaches it as recorded in Luke of the

New Testament, and Muhammad teaches it as recorded in the Quran; provides another example of Jesus and Muhammad being like 2 Rays of the Same Light!

It further demonstrates how they both were cognizant of G-d being THE ONE to pray to. At no time did G-d, The Creator of heaven and earth, ever have a need to pray to or call on Jesus or Muhammad for strength, consolation, or any kind of assistance; but regularly, and with sincere devotion, both **Jesus and Muhammad bowed down and prayed to G-d!**

JESUS AND MUHAMMAD TAUGHT: "THERE IS BUT ONE G-D", AND "TO BE KIND AND HAVE LOVE FOR YOUR FELLOW MAN"

*F*or good reason, I have selected key verses from the New Testament and the Quran, to illustrate the resemblance and similarity that exists in the teachings of Jesus and Muhammad. In my travels throughout the United States and abroad, I found that many people were amazingly surprised to hear, read, and learn that there was so much resemblance and likeness in their teaching.[1] As previously mentioned, the proximity and likeness of their teaching is not by coincidence or random incident, it is because Jesus and Muhammad are truly, 2 Rays of The Same Light!

In the following verses from the New Testament and the Quran, it is apparent that not only are Jesus and Muhammad advocating that there is only One G-d; interestingly after proclaiming this, they both immediately begin to address how each of us are to have love for our neighbor (our fellowman), as we love ourselves.[2]

Jesus teaching in the New Testament: Mark 12:28 -34

And one of the scribes came up and heard them disputing with one another, and seeing that he answered them well, asked him, "Which commandment is the first of all?" Jesus answered, "The first of all commandments is, 'Hear, O Israel: The Lord our God is One Lord; and you shall love the Lord your God with all your heart, all your soul, all your mind, and with all your strength, this is the first commandment.' The second is this, 'You shall love your neighbor as yourself.' There is no other commandment greater than these." And the scribe said to him, "You are right, Teacher; you have truly said that He is One, and there is no other but He; [3] and to love Him with all the heart, and with all the understanding, and with all the strength, and to love one's neighbor as oneself, is much more than all whole burnt offerings and sacrifices." [4] And when Jesus saw that he answered wisely, he said to him, "You are not far from the kingdom of God." And after that no one dared to ask him any question.

In these verses, Jesus establishes that (1) "the Lord our G-d, is one G-d", (2) "you shall love The Lord your G-d with all your heart, soul, mind, and strength", (3) "You shall love your neighbor as yourself", (4) "there is no other commandment greater than these". Then it is summarized by the scribe, that to accept no one else as "Lord" but The One G-d, and in fact to love G-d with all your heart (your emotions and affections), all your soul (your spiritual entity), all your mind (your intellect, thinking, and reasoning faculties), and all your strength (your physical health and material wealth) and to love your neighbor as you love yourself, is much more than all whole burnt offerings and sacrifices!

I find it interesting that as soon as Jesus mentions the Lord our G-d is One G-d, and that we are to love G-d with all our heart, soul, mind, and strength; he immediately mentions that we are to love our neighbor as we love ourselves. [5] The subject matter quickly shifts from our worship and sincere love for "The Lord our G-d who is One G-d", to how you are to love your neighbor as you love yourself. The moral and logic of Jesus teaching is that, after you accept the reality that "the Lord our G-d is One G-d", and you sincerely commit yourself to love

G-d with all your heart, all your mind, all your soul, and all your strength; then having love and kindness for your neighbor and fellow man becomes an automatic extension of your love for G-d, and therefore, a natural part of your social behavior. When you truly love G-d with all your heart, soul, mind, and strength; that level of G-d-consciousness creates a spiritual awakening inside of you, that makes showing love and kindness to your neighbor and fellow man come naturally!

Anyone can profess to believe "the Lord our G-d is One G-d", anyone can say, "Yes, I believe in G-d"; however, the proof is in the pudding! This is exactly why immediately after mentioning this, Jesus changes the focus of attention from how we are to love G-d with all our heart, mind, soul, and strength; to how we are to prove that by showing love and kindness to our neighbor and fellow man. In other words, the Lord our G-d, who is One G-d, is also The One who gave existence and purpose to every other human being on this earth besides you. We are all neighbors of each other! You say you love G-d, then prove it by showing love and kindness to your neighbor, who may or may not look like you, just as you love yourself! This is the litmus test not many people seem to pass.

Once again, the teaching of Muhammad from the Quran affirms and reiterates what Jesus taught, and it starts by reminding us of the love and kindness we should have for our parents first; after all, if we can't love and be kind to our parents who we do know, how can we have love and be kind to our neighbor who we do not know? The teaching of Muhammad is found in the Quran, chapter 17: 23 - 26. It reads as follows....

> Your Lord has decreed that you worship none but Him, and that you be kind to your parents; whether one or both of them attain old age in your life, say not to them a word of contempt, nor repel them, but address them in terms of honor; and out of kindness, lower to them the wing of humility, and say: "O my Lord, bestow on them Your Mercy even as they cherished me in childhood"; Your Lord knows best what is in your hearts: if you do deeds of righteousness, verily He is Most Forgiving to those who turn to Him again and again in true penitence; And render to your kindred their due rights, and also to those in need, and to the wayfarer: but squander not your wealth in the manner of a spendthrift.

Comparative Reflection

Interestingly, the New Testament verses taught by Jesus and these verses from the Quran taught by Muhammad, both begin by declaring emphatically, the Lord our G-d is One G-d, and that you worship none but Him. The fact that Jesus and Muhammad both start from this affirmation, should be an obvious "attention grabber" for anyone who carefully examines their teaching with impartiality. In Mark 12: 28-34 of the New Testament, Jesus began by saying "The Lord our G-d is One Lord". In the Quran, 17: 23-26, Muhammad's teaching began by saying, "Your Lord has decreed that you worship none but Him".

Jesus and Muhammad are not only similar in their message, but once again, their message progresses along the same line of spiritual logic and moral application. After advocating "The Lord our G-d is One Lord and we are to love Him with all our heart, mind, soul, and strength", Jesus quickly detours from that subject and makes a right turn on "love your neighbor as much as you love yourself" street!

Muhammad did the same thing! His teaching began by saying, "Your Lord has decreed that you worship none but G-d", then He quickly detours from that subject and makes a right turn on "be kind to your parents" street! He too, like Jesus, first establishes what should be the purity of our worship, which is the worship of "The Lord our G-d who is One". Then upon that principle, and from the moral obligation that principle imposes on us as servants of The Most High, we are directed as to how we are to love and be kind to our parents, our neighbor, and so forth.

Jesus directs our attention to love our neighbor as we love ourselves, Muhammad directs our attention to love and be kind to our parents. The author contends that, considering the normal propensities of human behavior; it is highly unlikely that anyone will love their neighbor nearly half as much as they love their self, if they can't even be loving and kind to their own parents who raised them.[5] It is for this reason the author further contends, the message of these verses in the Quran given to Muhammad, was to call man's attention back to the high regard and kindness we should have for our parents first; perhaps after this, we can do a better job of having love for our neighbor and fellow man! It begins at home with having gratitude, love, and showing true kindness to our parents who cherished us as children and nurtured us through our years of adolescence.

After describing the love, humility, and kindness we are to have for our parents, the teaching of Muhammad from the Quran goes on to say, "And render to your kindred (relatives) their due rights, and also to those in want, and to the wayfarer"! From these words of the Quran, we are directed to recognize the hierarchy and natural order of how our "regards" and acts of love and kindness are to be rendered. Muhammad's teaching is therefore consistent with the teaching of Jesus, because it reminds us like Jesus did, (1) that the Lord our G-d is One Lord, and we are to worship Him only (2) and that we are to love our neighbor as ourselves, by first starting with our parents and relatives who we do know, and then equally to our neighbors, those in want, and the wayfarers (people we meet in our travels) who we don't know!

The author contends once again that, the similarity and parallel that exists in these words taught by Jesus and Muhammad are not haphazard or by random coincidence, they are however, by the plan of The Lord our G-d, who is One Lord! The teaching of Muhammad that reminds us "to worship none but G-d, and to be kind to our parents, relatives, those in want, and the wayfarer we meet along the way of our travels"; is congruent and consistent with the teaching of Jesus that reminds us "The Lord our G-d is One Lord, and you shall love Him with all your heart, soul, mind and strength; and you shall love your neighbor as you love yourself". Let all the temples, churches, mosques, and all places of worship say AMEN!

As an additional reference from the Quran that Muhammad taught, which further resembles and corroborates the teaching of Jesus, consider the following verse from the Quran 4: 36-38

"Worship Allah (G-d), and join not any partners with Him; and do good to your parents, kinsfolk, orphans, those in need, neighbors who are near, neighbors who are strangers, the companion by your side, the wayfarer you meet, and what your right hands possess: for Allah (G-d) loves not the arrogant, the vainglorious; Nor those who are stingy and enjoin stinginess on others, or hide the bounties which Allah (G-d) has bestowed on them; for We have prepared for those who resist faith a punishment that steeps them in contempt; Nor those who spend of their substance, to be seen of men, but have no faith in G-d and the Last Day: if anyone take the evil one for their intimate, what a dreadful intimate he is".

This passage from the Quran that Muhammad taught, further resembles the message of Jesus regarding the worship of G-d alone and having love for our neighbor, as we love ourselves. In fact, this verse from the Quran further extrapolates the idea of "concern and love for our neighbor, as we love ourselves", that Jesus taught. This verse that Muhammad taught is detailed, and directs us as Jesus did, to worship G-d only, and not join any associates or partners with G-d; and to be good to (1) our parents, (2) relatives, (3) orphans, (4) to those in need, (5) neighbors who are near, (6) neighbors who are strangers, (7) the companion by your side, (8) the wayfarer you meet in your travels, (9) what your right hand possess, (10) G-d loves not the arrogant and vainglorious, (11) G-d loves not those who are stingy and who encourages stinginess to others, (12) G-d does not love those who spend of their substance in order to be seen by others.

In each of these scenarios described in the Quran that Muhammad taught, there is equally similar attention and address given from Jesus in the New Testament. The author finds it interesting, in fact, joyously encouraging, that the teaching of Muhammad from the Quran not only reiterates Jesus's message of love for our neighbor as we love ourselves; it goes even further and illustrates the expectation that G-d has of each of us, to be considerate and show kindness and regard in the different scenarios of a "neighbor"!

JESUS AND MUHAMMAD'S PARABLE: REMEMBER G-D WITH YOUR WEALTH AND MATERIAL POSSESIONS!

Jesus and Muhammad both recognized that wealth and material possessions are gifts and favors that G-d bestows on each of us, and that we should always be grateful and remember G-d with whatever we have. However, they both knew the greed, selfishness, and vanity that often comes with material affluence, as well as the tendency many have of acquiring material possessions for the sake of boasting and showing off. From the parable of the New Testament (Luke 12: 16-21) that Jesus taught, and from the parable in the Quran (18: 32-44) that Muhammad taught, you will see that with parables, they were both addressing the same ideals and values.[1]

The New Testament parable taught by Jesus (Luke 12: 16-21)

And he spoke a parable to them saying, "The ground of a certain rich man brought forth plentifully, and he thought within himself, saying, What shall I do, because I have no room where to bestow my fruits? And he said, This will I do: I will pull down my barns, and build greater, and there will I bestow all my fruits and all my goods. And I will say to my soul, Soul, thou have much goods laid up for many years; take thine ease, eat, drink, and be merry. But G-d said to him, Thou

51

fool, this night thy soul shall be required of thee; then whose shall those things be, which thou have provided? So is he that lay up treasure for himself, and is not rich toward G-d".[2]

The parable taught by Muhammad from the Quran (18: 32-44)

"Set forth to them the parable of two men: for one of them We provided two gardens of grapevines and surrounded them with date palms: in between the two We placed cornfields. Each of those gardens brought forth its produce, and failed not in the least therein: in the midst of them We caused a river to flow. Abundant was the produce this man had: he said to his companion in the course of a mutual argument: "more wealth have I than you, and more honor and power in my following of men". He went into his garden in a "state of mind" unjust to his soul: He said, "I deem not that this will ever perish". "Nor do I deem that the Hour of Judgement will ever come: even if I am brought back to my Lord, I shall surely find there something better in exchange".[3] His companion said to him in the course of the argument with him: "Do you deny Him who created you out of dust, then out of a sperm drop, then fashioned you into a man? But I think for my part, that He is Allah, my Lord, and none shall I associate with my Lord. Why did you not, as you went into your garden, say, "Allah's will be done. There is no power but with Allah! If you see me less than you in wealth and sons, it may be that my Lord will give me something better than your garden, and that He will send on your garden thunderbolts by way of reckoning from heaven, making it but slippery sand!, or the water of the garden will run off underground so that you will never be able to find it". So, his fruits and enjoyment were encompassed with ruin, and he remained twisting and turning his hands over what he had spent on his property, which had now tumbled to pieces to its very foundations. And he could only say, "Woe is me!, would that I had never ascribed partners to my Lord and Cherisher! Nor had he numbers to help him against Allah, nor was he able to defend himself. There, the only protection comes from Allah, The True One. He is the Best to reward, and the Best to give success.[4]

SIMILARITIES IN JESUS AND MUHAMMAD'S PARABLE

There are several key points shared in the parable taught   by Jesus that are equally shared in the parable taught by Muhammad. The significance of these shared key points, and the fact that both Jesus and Muhammad's parables are related in similar context and format, is further evidence of the likeness of their moral intelligence and spiritual outlook.[5]

The parable taught by Jesus involved a rich man whose land brought forth plentifully with fruits and goods. His harvest was so plentiful, he thought to himself to tear down the barn he had, so that he could build a bigger barn to store all his fruits and goods.

Engrossed with feelings of accomplishment and security, as well as feelings of egocentricity, conceit, and self-indulgence; he said to his own soul, "Soul, you have much goods laid up for many years, take thine ease, eat, drink, and be merry". Little did he know, that very night G-d would take his soul and say to him, "Thou fool, this night your soul will be required of thee (this night you shall die), then whose shall those things be, which thou have provided? So is he that lays up treasure for himself but is not rich toward G-d".

At no time did this man ever express any thanks or gratitude to G-d for his abundance of harvest. He never stopped to consider that his prosperity was not only a blessing, but that it was also a testing! He did not realize that with every blessing that G-d bestows, there is a quiz and test that comes along with it, to see how we will behave and conduct ourselves! Unfortunately, this man failed his test! His material affluence got the best of him. He became consumed with his own self-interest to the extent that (1) he never paused to consider, thank, and praise G-d for what he had acquired, (2) he never expressed any care or concern about anyone else but his self, (3) he thought of himself as so safe and secure from ever having to need, that he said to his own soul, "eat, drink, and be merry", and (4) he was so preoccupied with laying up treasures for his self, but had no thought of what he could do to be rich with G-d.

The parable from the Quran that Muhammad taught involved two men, one who was abundantly rich and subsequently enjoyed high status in society from the fruits of his two gardens; the other was a man who did not possess a garden, but what he did possess, was in fact more valuable than the material wealth and social status of the man with two gardens. The Quran describes the rich mans' two gardens as being very abundant with grapes, date palms, and cornfields. In addition, it says that in the midst of his two gardens, G-d caused a river to flow. So not only was this man favored with two productive gardens, G-d caused a river to flow in the midst of them to provide agricultural support. During the course of a mutual disagreement between the two men, the man with the two flourishing gardens said to the other man, "I have much more wealth than you and much more power in my following of men". The Quran further states that, like the man in the parable of Jesus, this man went into his garden in a "state of mind" unjust to his soul, and in fact said, "I deem not that this will ever perish". He further boasted, "Nor do I deem that the Hour of Judgement will ever come: even if I am brought back to my Lord, I shall surely find there something better in exchange".

At this point of the dialogue, the other man attempted to appeal to his conscience. He did this by asking him, "Do you deny Him who created you out of dust, then out of a sperm drop, then developed you into a man?" [4] He goes on to say, "But I think for my part that He is Allah, my Lord, and none shall I associate with my Lord; why did you not, as you went into your garden, say: "Allah's Will be done! There is no power but with Allah! If you see me less than you in wealth and sons, it may be that my Lord will give me something better than your garden, and that He will send on your garden thunderbolts by way of reckoning from heaven, making it but slippery sand; or the water of the garden will run off underground so that you will never be able to find it"

The parable begins closure by stating that the rich man fruits and enjoyment were encompassed with total ruin, and he remained in a state of anguish and sorrow over what he had spent on his property, that was now completely destroyed!

In both parables taught by Jesus and Muhammad, the circumstance, setting, and moral lesson is quite similar. The parables of Jesus and Muhammad involve a man who was materially rich from the produce of his garden, subsequently both men enjoyed substantial wealth and prosperity. In addition to material prosperity, the man mentioned in the Quran boasted of having more social prestige and power in his following of men. The parables of Jesus and Muhammad describe men who unfortunately became "wrapped up" in material affluence but gave no recognition to where their blessings came from.

The parables of both Jesus and Muhammad also describe men who were blinded by conceit, egocentricity, the over-dose of pride, and the inordinate love of having material affluence at the expense of losing their very own soul! Last but most important, the parables of both Jesus and Muhammad conclude with the reminder that G-d is The One who holds the keys that can either open or close the door to true happiness and ultimate success! Once again, the teachings of Jesus and Muhammad pleasantly shake hands and illustrate profound likeness and similarity, this time in the form of parables!

JESUS TAUGHT BEATITUDES ON THE MOUNTAIN
MUHAMMAD TAUGHT BEATITUDES ON THE MOUNTAIN

*I*n the process of researching the New Testament and the Quran for common themes and similarities in the message of Jesus and Muhammad, and paying attention to unique details such as time and place, the author found it interesting that the place where both Jesus and Muhammad delivered perhaps one of their most historic and profound sermons, was a mountain! One of the significant features of a mountain as a location, is that it provides a large base area for multitudes of people to gather and listen, unlike a smaller temple or other house of worship. The specific name of the mountain from which Jesus spoke is not mentioned in our reference (Matthew 5: 1-20), however our reference does mention that multitudes of people from Galilee, Decapolis, Jerusalem, and even from Jordan, had followed him there to hear his teaching. This address given by Jesus is commonly referred to as "The Sermon on The Mount", also called, "The Beatitudes"! According to the New Testament, Matthew 5: 1-20, we read...

And seeing the multitudes, he (Jesus) went up into a mountain: and when he was set, his disciples came unto him: and he opened his mouth and taught them saying, "Blessed are the poor in spirit: for theirs is the kingdom of heaven. Blessed are they that mourn, for they shall be comforted. Blessed are the meek, for they shall inherit the earth. Blessed are they that which do hunger and thirst after righteousness, for they shall be filled. Blessed are the merciful, for they shall obtain mercy. Blessed are the pure in heart, for they shall see G-d. Blessed are the peacemakers, for they shall be called the children of G-d. Blessed are they which are persecuted for righteousness sake, for theirs is the kingdom of heaven. Blessed are you, when men shall revile, and persecute you and shall say all manner of evil against you falsely, for my sake.

Rejoice and be exceedingly glad, for great is your reward in heaven: for so persecuted they the prophets which were before you. You are the salt of the earth: but if the salt has lost his savour, wherewith shall it be salted? It is therefore good for nothing but to be cast out, and to be trodden under the foot of men. You are the light of the world. A city that is set on a hill cannot be hid. Neither do men light a candle, and put it under a bushel, but on a candlestick: and it giveth light unto all that are in the house. Let your light so shine before men, that they may see your good works, and glorify your father which is in Heaven.

Think not that I am come to destroy the law or the prophets: I am not come to destroy, but to fulfill. For verily I say unto you, till heaven and earth pass, one jot or one tittle shall in no wise pass from the law, till all be fulfilled. Whoever therefore shall break one of these least commandments, and shall teach men so, he shall be called the least in the kingdom of heaven: but whoever shall do and teach them, the same shall be called great in the kingdom of heaven. For I say unto you, that unless your righteousness exceeds the righteousness of the scribes and Pharisees, you shall in no case enter into the kingdom of heaven".

While there is much more that Jesus taught in his "Sermon on the Mount", for the sake of brevity the author has selected verses 1-20 for the express purpose of emphasizing once again, that there are many diverse themes and topics that were addressed by both Jesus and Muhammad, but the two common threads that consistently stands out in all their teaching is, (1) moral sensitivity and (2) spiritual consciousness! As such, it is imperative that we reflect on these "Beatitudes" delivered by Jesus in his "Sermon on the Mount", for they contain valuable "character-shaping precepts" that everyone should embrace. We will revisit the sermon delivered by Jesus momentarily, but first let us now look at the sermon that was given by Muhammad, which was also delivered on a mountain!

The name of this historic mountain is called Mount Arafat, located approximately 12 miles southeast of Mecca. The reference source for this sermon however is not the Quran, it is the "hadiths". You may recall it was mentioned earlier in this book, the "hadiths" are a collection of authentic traditions and sayings reported of Muhammad. The Quran is the revelation that G-d revealed to Muhammad, just as G-d had revealed the Gospel to Jesus about 570 years before. The "hadiths" however, are a collection of authentic traditions and sayings of Muhammad originating from his own personal thoughts and spiritual observations, as he was "taught, enlightened, and educated" by the revelation of the Quran. The "hadiths" therefore, are thought provoking observations and inspiring expressions originating from himself.[1]

It is from these thought-provoking observations and inspiring expressions where the "Last Sermon and Farewell Address" of Muhammad is found. As it was previously mentioned in the New Testament, Jesus had a tremendously large multitude of people who followed him to the mountain where he delivered the "Beatitudes", not surprisingly, Muhammad also had a tremendously large multitude of people that accompanied him as well! This incredibly large multitude of people had accompanied Muhammad on Hajj (The Sacred Pilgrimage) and had gathered at Mount Arafat where he delivered what is historically referred to as, "The Last Sermon and Farewell Address". After thanking and praising G-d, he said,

"O People, lend me an attentive ear, for I know not whether after this year, I shall ever be amongst you again. Therefore, listen to what I am saying to you very carefully, and take these words to those who could not be here today.

O People, just as you regard this month, day, and city as Sacred, so should you regard the life and property of every person as a sacred trust. Return the goods entrusted to you to their rightful owners. Hurt no one so that no one would want to hurt you. Remember that you will indeed meet your LORD, and that HE will indeed reckon all of your deeds. ALLAH has forbidden you to take usury (interest), therefore all interest obligations shall henceforth be waived. Your capital, however, is yours to keep. You will neither inflict nor suffer any inequity.

Beware of Satan, for the safety of your way of life. He has lost all hope that he will ever be able to lead you astray in big things, so beware of following him in small things.

O People, it is true that you have certain rights with your women, but they also have rights over you! Remember that you have taken them as your wives only under Allah's trust and with His permission. If they abide by your right, then to them belongs the right to be fed and clothed in kindness. Do treat your women well and be kind to them for they are your partners and committed helpers.

O People, listen to me in earnest, worship ALLAH, say your five daily prayers, fast during the month of Ramadan, and give your wealth in Zakat. Perform Hajj if you can afford to.

All mankind is from Adam and Eve, an Arab has no superiority over a non-Arab, nor does a non-Arab have any superiority over an Arab; also, a white has no superiority over a black, nor does a black have any superiority over a white, except in G-d consciousness and good action! Learn that every Muslim is a brother to every other Muslim, and that the Muslims constitute one brotherhood. Nothing shall be legitimate to a Muslim which belongs to a fellow Muslim, unless it was given freely and willingly. Do not, therefore, do injustice to yourselves.

Remember, one day you will appear before ALLAH and answer for your deeds! So beware, do not stray from the path of righteousness after I am gone. Reason well, therefore, O People, and understand the words which I am conveying to you. I leave behind me two things, the QURAN and my example, and if you follow these you will never go astray!

All those who listen to me shall pass on my words to others, and those to others again; and it may be that the last ones may understand my words better than those who are listening to me directly. Be my witness, O ALLAH, that I have conveyed your message to the people".

The author encourages each person to continue using "unbiased" inductive observation and sound deductive reasoning, as we now begin to compare and analyze the sermons of Jesus and Muhammad. To see and truly understand what is clearly apparent on the surface, and intelligently deduce what is implied beneath the surface; it is imperative to proceed with a mind that is open, objective, and equitable.

For example, a Biology professor dissects a frog for a demonstration before his students in the laboratory, identifying major organs, muscles, tissues, etc., each step of the way. Likewise, a Chemistry instructor closely examines and identifies for his students the similar properties of two different gases such as Helium and Argon. Surprisingly, the students learn that Helium and Argon are both odorless, colorless, tasteless, nonflammable under normal conditions, and finally, they learn that Helium and Argon both belong to a special group of elements in chemistry called, "the Noble Gases". The author contends that there is a similar "nobility" in the comparative properties of Jesus and Muhammad.[2]

SIMILAR PROPERTIES IN JESUS AND MUHAMMADS' SERMON

For starters, it is interesting to note that the sermons of Jesus and Muhammad both took place at the location of a mountain. On the surface, for some, this fun fact may appear to be trivial and not that significant. However, those who give merit to noteworthy "hints and clues" find it not only a fun fact, but in fact ponder the spiritual significance in multitudes of people gathered at a mountain site, listening to a thought-provoking, heart-felt sermon from Jesus and Muhammad. The location of a temple, synagogue, or mosque, though highly sacred, imposes the feeling of one being somewhat confined by space and is considered static. The location of a mountain however is not static and has a direct connection with the wonders of nature (sunlight, breeze of the wind, possibly observation of birds, etc.).

Then we have the setting, in the case of Jesus, we are reminded in Matthew of the New Testament that multitudes of people were following him. It says that Jesus went all about Galilee teaching in their synagogues, preaching the gospel of the kingdom. It says that his fame went throughout all of Syria, and that people with diverse diseases and torments were brought to him; those possessed with evil intent, those who were lunatic (mentally disabled), and even those with palsy (muscle paralysis); and he healed them! It further says that great multitudes of people followed him from Galilee, Decapolis, Jerusalem, Judea, and even as far as Jordan. Then, as the multitudes of people followed him, it says he went up into a mountain, and there he began his Sermon starting with "The Beatitudes".

In the case of Muhammad, we are reminded in the hadiths that multitudes of people had come to perform their Hajj (Sacred Pilgrimage) in Mecca. As you may know, Hajj is the sacred pilgrimage where people from many diverse parts of the world come to partake in the ceremonial rites of prayers, symbolic gestures of sacrifice, purity of worship, spiritual rejuvenation, rejection of sin and evil, commemoration of Prophet Abraham, and the engage of acquainting oneself with other fellow worshipers from diverse ethnicities and races, especially on the day of going to Arafat. On the day of this historic address, some historians give an estimate of up to 30,000 followers that had gathered in the Uranah valley of Mount Arafat, to hear this historic sermon of Muhammad·

Jesus begins his sermon first with the 9 Beatitudes

(1) Blessed are the poor in spirit, for theirs' is the kingdom of heaven.
(2) Blessed are they that mourn, for they shall be comforted.
(3) Blessed are the meek, for they shall inherit the earth.
(4) Blessed are they which do hunger and thirst after righteousness, for they shall be filled.
(5) Blessed are the merciful, for they shall obtain mercy.
(6) Blessed are the pure in heart, for they shall see G-d.
(7) Blessed are the peacemakers, for they shall be called the children of G-d.
(8) Blessed are they which are persecuted for righteousness sake, for theirs' is the kingdom of heaven.
(9) Blessed are you, when men shall revile you and persecute you, and say all manner of evil against you falsely, for my sake.

Muhammad praises and thanks G-d, and then begins

(1) Listen closely to my words, convey them to those not here.

(2) Regard the life and property of every person as a sacred trust.

(3) Hurt no one, so that no one would want to hurt you.

(4) Remember, you will meet your Lord and He will reckon all   of your deeds.

(5) G-d has forbidden you to take (usury) interest, therefore all interest obligations shall be henceforth waived.

(6) It is true that you have rights with regards to your women, but they also have rights over you.

(7) Treat your women well and be kind to them, for they are your partners and committed helpers.

(8) Listen to me earnestly, worship Allah (G-d), say your 5 daily prayers, fast during the month of Ramadan, give your wealth in charity, make Hajj if you can afford to.

(9) All mankind is from Adam and Eve; an Arab has no superiority over a non-Arab, nor does a non-Arab have any superiority over an Arab; also, a white has no superiority over a black, nor does a black have any superiority over a white, except in God consciousness and good actions!

SHARED VALUES & MORAL PRECEPTS: 2 SERMONS, ONE AIM

The relational significance in the "Beatitudes" of Jesus and the "Beatitudes" of Muhammad is not only recognizable to the average 7th grader, but it is also quite profound, so profound that, after reading this section of the book, many will be compelled by reason and logic to modify their former views in light of new introduced perspectives. When the average person is introduced with new information that may have a relation with something

65

they previously thought or understood; most people use their "reasoning abilities" to see what connection or relation possibly exists. If they see a sensible relationship between the two, their next step is to better understand how the new and the previous share similar properties. A prime example we all can relate to is how we first learned the operations of addition and subtraction, and once understood, we were then introduced to the functions of multiplication and division. Like-wise, it is only after we understand the properties of multiplication and division that we can even begin to understand the properties of algebra and more complexed mathematical applications.

The author contends that just as there is an association and logical relation between addition and subtraction to multiplication and division, likewise there is an ethical and logical relation between the "Beatitudes" of Jesus and the "Moral-Social Precepts of Muhammad.

In my opinion, the "Beatitudes" taught by Jesus are "prerequisites" and foundational "character building blocks" aimed at refining and re-establishing the human soul to be what G-d wants of each individual person. The "Beatitudes" taught by Muhammad aim at properly counseling and directing those same individuals who have been refined and re-born with a new G-d-loving spirit from the Beatitudes; to now know how to co-exist and interact with other people in the broader society, in a manner that is pleasing to G-d and considerate of their fellow man.

While the broader society is composed of individual persons, the broader society is therefore more dynamic than the individual person. The individual is just that, one individual entity. The broader society however, is composed of the opposite gender, neighbors that are near, neighbors that are far, numerous cultures and diverse ethnic groups, children, the elderly, orphans, the needy, widows, blue-collar workers, white-collar workers, Jews, Muslims, Christians, Buddhist, Hindus, other religious affiliates, etc. and so forth. On one mountain, we had Jesus teaching the Beatitudes, on another mountain, we had Muhammad teaching the Moral-Social Precepts. One primarily appealing to the cleansing and reformation of the individual, the other primarily appealing to their moral and social responsibilities in the community and broader society; both however with inference to the other. The sermon from Jesus and the sermon from Muhammad is the perfect appeal to the microcosm (individual) and the macrocosm (broader society). [4]

Beatitudes of Jesus

Blessed are the poor in spirit, theirs is the kingdom of heaven.

Blessed are they that mourn, they shall be comforted.

Blessed are the meek, for they shall inherit the earth.

Blessed are they which do hunger and thirst after righteousness; for they shall be filled.

Blessed are the merciful, for they shall obtain mercy.

Beatitudes of Muhammad

Regard the life and property of every person as sacred.

Hurt no one so that no one would want to hurt you.

You will meet your Lord and He will reckon all your deeds.

You have rights over women, but they also have rights over you!

Treat your women well and be Kind to them, for they are your partners and committed helpers.

Beatitudes of Jesus

Blessed are the pure in heart, for they shall see G-d!

Blessed are the peacemakers, they shall be called the children of G-d!

Blessed are they which are persecuted for righteousness sake, for theirs is the kingdom of heaven!

You are the salt of the earth, but if salt has lost its savor, wherewith shall it be salted? It is good for nothing, but to be cast out and trodden under the foot of men.

You are the light of the world. A city that is set on a hill cannot be hid. Let your light shine before men, that they may see your good works and glorify your Father which is in heaven.

Unless your righteousness exceeds that of the scribes and Pharisees, you will not enter the kingdom of Heaven!

Beatitudes of Muhammad

Worship Allah (G-d), say your 5 daily prayers, fast during the month of Ramadan, give in charity, make Hajj if you can.

G-d has forbidden you to take usury (interest), therefore all interest obligations shall be henceforth waived.

All mankind is from Adam and Eve; an Arab has no superiority over a non-Arab, nor does a non-Arab have any superiority over an Arab; also a white has no superiority over a black, nor does a black have any superiority over a white, except in G-d consciousness and good actions!

Do not stray from the path of righteousness after I am gone!

All who are listening to me shall pass my words on to others, and those to others, again, it may be that the last ones may understand my words better than those who are listening now.

Be my witness O Allah, that I have conveyed your message to the people!

THE PROOF IS IN THE PUDDING

The sermons of Jesus and Muhammad are not only mutually compatible with each other; they also have a reciprocating connection to each other. The author contends in addition, that the Beatitudes of Jesus are "prerequisites" for the Beatitudes taught by Muhammad. In other words, the human person must first be in tune with the "character building virtues" that Jesus so excellently taught, before they are morally and intellectually capable of living by the standard Muhammad taught. The author furthermore contends that the Moral-Social precepts taught by Muhammad, are ethics and values consistent with the teachings of Jesus. To each of G-d's esteemed servants, there are distinct tasks and objectives that they were missioned to fulfill. The message that each of G-d's servants taught, corroborates and reinforces what those prior to them taught. In other words, certain truths were meant to be advocated at certain times and places, in preparation for other truths and moral precepts that would come later, as the society of man expanded.[1]

The Beatitudes of Jesus were meant to develop and cultivate within the human person the right virtues and attitudes, that would gradually prepare society to evolve and graduate into the Moral-Social Precepts taught by Muhammad. The proof is in the pudding. Muhammad addressed in his sermon, volatile subjects that became major issues in the history of man. There are 2 major issues that, according to what is recorded in the New Testament, Jesus never explicitly addressed or directly taught about. If you search through the Gospels according to Matthew, Mark, Luke, and John; you will not find a single moment where Jesus specifically addressed the subject of the status and equality of women, or the issue of ethnic prejudice and racism. In the history of the United States for example, these 2 matters became critical and major issues that oppressed both the civic rights of women and the human rights of African Americans through slavery, and afterwards through the system of Jim Crow legislature. This observation is not meant to imply that Jesus over looked or forgot anything, nor is it meant to suggest that Jesus fell short in any way. On the contrary, and as recently stated, it is important to understand that certain truths and moral precepts were meant to be preached and advocated at certain points in the history of man; while more and other specific truths and moral precepts were meant to be preached and advocated at much later times.[2]

The kind and fair treatment of women, and the racial-ethnic equality of man addressed by Muhammad in his Last Sermon, should be of key interest and high consideration to the attentive reader. Throughout history, women were considered as being not equal to men, subsequently deemed inferior, and therefore were not afforded equal entitlements. Their civic rights, communal entitlements, and especially their social status throughout history, has always been met with resistance and opposition. Their on-going struggle for fair treatment, equal entitlements, civic and domestic respect, has been ubiquitous throughout the history of every culture. Not surprisingly in the authors' view, Muhammad was not only speaking to the dismal reality of his era, with regards to the fair and considerate treatment of women. Equally and more prophetically, he was speaking to the future when he addressed the multitudes of people stating, "You have rights over women, but they also have rights over you (men), therefore treat your women well and be kind to them, for they are your partners and committed helpers".[3]

For man to be equitable, kind, fair, and considerate of women as taught by Muhammad, he must first humble himself to G-d and pass "Beatitudes 101" as taught by Jesus, "Blessed are the meek, for they shall inherit the earth" and "Blessed are they which do hunger and thirst after righteousness, for they shall be filled".[4]

The racial-ethnic equality of man addressed by Muhammad in his Last Sermon, is another critical issue that should be of major significance to the observant reader.

By advocating that an Arab has no superiority over a non-Arab, nor does a non-Arab have any superiority over an Arab, and that a White has no superiority over a Black, nor does a Black have any superiority over a White, except in G-d-consciousness and good actions; Muhammad was addressing and identifying perhaps one of the greatest dilemmas and travesties of equality and justice the world has ever known. Racism and ethnic superiority complexes have not only divided humanity along the lines of color and ethnicity; it has continuously plagued our society to the core and fostered an atmosphere where superiority and inferiority is judged by race and ethnicity, instead of the content of character, as expressed by Dr. Martin Luther King Jr. Muhammad was very much aware of this overt and subliminal dilemma, as well as the "psychological scars" that both the presumed superior and alleged inferior carry.[5]

Therefore, in consistency with the Beatitudes that Jesus taught, Muhammad admonished the multitudes of people in his Last Sermon to not judge superiority and inferiority by race, color, or ethnicity, but instead to judge superiority and inferiority by who has more G-d-consciousness and right conduct! Once again, and as would be expected, you must pass "Beatitudes 101" as taught by Jesus, before you can pass "Beatitudes 102" as taught by Muhammad! In other words, you must be meek, pure in heart, hungering, yearning, and in fact thirsting after righteousness as Jesus taught; before you can even begin to walk by the Moral-Social Precepts Muhammad taught; particularly the fair, kind, and equitable treatment of women, and the practice of not casting superiority and inferiority complexes based on race, color, and ethnicity.

Not surprisingly, just as many after Jesus failed to carry on and walk by the "Beatitudes" that he taught, many after Muhammad also failed to carry on and walk by the Moral-Social Precepts that he taught.[6] Presently, there are many still who claim to be followers of Jesus and Muhammad, but much of their thinking and actions are far from and contrary to the message Jesus and Muhammad taught, and how they ACTUALLY lived. Fortunately, however, there are many people in society and around the world, at every level of human interest and endeavor, who claim to follow Jesus and Muhammad, and they do in fact exemplify the excellence of the

Beatitudes taught by Jesus and the excellence of the Moral-Social Precepts taught by Muhammad in a commendable way. Family, friends, co-workers, neighbors, in fact anyone who interacts with them, can immediately recognize "the light" emanating from their words and deeds.

For this reason, the author advised each reader earlier in this book, to not judge or measure Islam and Christianity by the character of the people who call themselves Muslims or Christians; but rather, judge and measure the people who call themselves Muslims and Christians, by the standard and moral example Jesus and Muhammad set! Also, despite the misdeeds and wayward actions that many have done while claiming to be followers of Jesus and Muhammad, that are contrary to what Jesus and Muhammad practiced and taught; it would be not only unfair but a major over sight, to not recognize the mutual complement and synergy that exists in their teaching and moral example.

From the virtues of being meek, pure in heart, thirsting and hungering for righteousness as Jesus taught; to regarding the life and property of other people as sacred, being kind, considerate, and recognizing the rights and equal status of women, and not judging superiority by race, color, and ethnicity as Muhammad taught; once again, and this time as taught while standing on two different mountain sites, Jesus and Muhammad are like 2 Rays shining from the Same Light!

JESUS AND MUHAMMAD: PROPHETS OF THE ONE G-D

*A*nother shared feature of Jesus and Muhammad is that they were both Prophets sent by the One G-d, subsequently they were both given scripture (revelation). The revelation sent to Jesus was the Gospel, commonly referred to as the "Good News". The revelation sent to Muhammad was the "Quran". There are several references in the Gospel, according to the New Testament, where Jesus refers to himself as a Prophet. Likewise, there are several references in the Quran where Jesus and Muhammad are both described as Prophets, and in fact are listed among many other Prophets and Messengers sent by G-d.

The author contends that the significance of Jesus and Muhammad being Prophets sent from The One G-d has at least three notable implications. (1) If Jesus and Muhammad were both Prophets of G-d, that means they were both "inspired" from the same source (The Lord Thy G-d who is One), (2) if Jesus and Muhammad were both Prophets sent from the One G-d, that means that the Gospel that was revealed to Jesus, is relevant to the Quran that was revealed to Muhammad, and (3) if Jesus and Muhammad were both Prophets sent from the One G-d, that means that Jesus and Muhammad should not be viewed as opponents or contenders, but instead, they should be viewed as two men chosen and guided by the same One G-d, having not identical but complementary missions, fulfilling The Will and Purpose of He that sent them both.[1]

To better understand the relation and synergy of Jesus and Muhammad as prophets of the One G-d, reflect for a moment on the words of Jesus as he addressed his relation to Prophet Moses, who was before him.

In Matthew 5: 17-20 of the New Testament Jesus says:

"Think not that I have come to destroy the Law or the prophets; I am not come to destroy, but to fulfill. For verily I say unto you, till heaven and earth pass, one jot or tittle shall in no wise pass from the Law, till all be fulfilled. Whosoever therefore shall break one of these least commandments, and shall teach men so, he shall be called the least in the kingdom of heaven: but whosoever shall do and teach them, the same shall be called great in the kingdom of heaven. For I say unto you, unless your righteousness exceeds the righteousness of the scribes and the Pharisees, you shall in no way enter into the kingdom of heaven".

Jesus was quite familiar with the poor in spirit and unlearned among the citizens in nearby towns and surrounding villages. Jesus was also privy to the dubious mindset held by the religious leadership of his day, primarily the doctors of law, the rabbis, and high priest. In addition, Jesus was also aware that some people, especially among the scribes and the Pharisees, thought that he was seeking to do away with or deviate from the Law and statutes established by Prophet Moses who was before him. He did not want people to view him as deviating from the Law or contending in any way with what was established by Prophet Moses, and so he said "think not that I have come to destroy the Law or the Prophets".[2]

Jesus further stated that "until heaven and earth pass, one jot or tittle shall in no wise pass from the law, till all be fulfilled". Therefore, suffice it to say, as from these words uttered by Jesus, there is no ground or support for viewing Jesus as doing away with, underscoring, or underestimating the status of his fore runner, Prophet Moses or "The Law" given to Prophet Moses. In other words, he wanted people to understand the relational significance of him and Prophet Moses, as well as appreciate the synergy that exists between the Law given to Moses and the Gospel given to him.[3]

In like manner, there is relational significance in the teaching of Prophet Jesus and Prophet Muhammad. Having been sent by and inspired by, The Lord Thy G-d who is One G-d, they both admonished the people of their day to serve and worship The Lord Thy G-d who is One G-d, to love and be considerate of your neighbor as yourself, and to be compassionate and mindful of the less fortunate. They both led by example by devoutly praying to G-d and teaching their people to be devout and pray as well. They both fasted, as a means of drawing nearer to G-d and out of mindfulness of the poor and those in need· As Prophets sent by and guided by, The Lord Thy G-d who is One G-d, they both had a natural "affinity" towards the poor, down-trodden, unlearned, and socially impoverished in society. The New Testament, Luke 4: 14 - 20 says:

And Jesus returned in the power of the Spirit into Galilee: and there went out a fame of him through all the region round about; And he taught in their synagogues, being glorified of all; And he came to Nazareth, where he had been brought up: and, as his custom was, he went into the synagogue on the Sabbath day, and stood up to read; And there was delivered unto him the book of the Prophet Esaias, and when he had opened the book, he found the place where it was written, " The Spirit of the Lord is upon me, because He has anointed me to preach the gospel to the poor; He has sent me to heal the brokenhearted, to preach deliverance to the captives, and recovering of sight to the blind, and to set at liberty them that are bruised, and to preach the acceptable year of the Lord"; And he closed the book and gave it again to the attendant, and sat down; And the eyes of all of them in the synagogue were fastened on him.

The author considers it highly significant that, when Jesus went to the synagogue and was presented with the book of prophet Esaias to read, he knew exactly where he wanted to read from, to convey the message he wanted to impart. He chose such words spoken by prophet Esaias that also described his own unique role and prophetic mission. All that were present in the synagogue listened attentively as Jesus spoke.

Prophet Jesus began by saying "The Spirit of The Lord is upon me, because He has anointed me to preach the gospel to the poor; He has sent me to heal the brokenhearted, to preach deliverance to the captives, and recovery of sight to the blind, to set at liberty them that are bruised, and to preach the acceptable year of the Lord". Think about that for a moment! Consider the social status of those who were often present in the synagogue when Jesus taught. He would be speaking to the Doctors of Law, the rabbis, scribes, Pharisees, Sadducees, and other high priests; those considered among the elite and higher echelon. He clearly states that his primary attention is to the (1) poor, (2) brokenhearted, (3) captives, (4) the spiritually blind, and (5) those who are socially "bruised".

Although approximately 769 miles away from and 570 years apart, Prophet Muhammad comes along and complements this teaching of Prophet Jesus in several places of the Quran. For example, in the Quran 2: 177, we read...

"It is not righteousness that you turn your faces towards East or West; but it is righteousness to believe in Allah(G-d) and the Last Day, and the Angels, and the Book, and the Messengers, and to spend out of your substance and out of love for Him(G-d), for your kin, for the orphans, for the needy, for the wayfarer, for those who ask, and for the ransom of slaves; to be steadfast in prayer, and practice regular charity; to fulfill the contracts which you have made, and to be firm and patient in pain or suffering and adversity; and throughout all periods of panic. Such are the people of truth, the G-d-fearing"!

In this verse from the Quran that was revealed to Muhammad, we find teaching that resembles what Jesus expressed as recorded in the New Testament. Jesus gives specific attention to the (1) poor, (2) brokenhearted, (3) captives, (4) the spiritually blind, and (5) those who are socially bruised.

In the verse from the Quran that Muhammad taught, we find (1) your kin, (2) the orphans, (3) the needy, (4) the wayfarer, (5) those who ask, and (6) the ransom of slaves.

Without debating semantics, the author contends that the poor and brokenhearted that Jesus spoke of, are at least proximal and comparable to the needy, the orphans, and those who ask, that Muhammad spoke of. The logic being, the needy, the orphans, and those who ask that Muhammad spoke of, share the same conditions and characteristics of the poor and brokenhearted that Jesus spoke of. Likewise, the captives, spiritually blind, and those bruised that Jesus spoke of, are also proximal and comparable to the "slaves" that Muhammad spoke of. Please remember, the term "slavery" has both literal and suggestive implications, as well as physical and psychological conditions and effects. Jesus said he wanted to preach deliverance to the captives and set at liberty those that are bruised. I think we all would agree that the slave mentioned by Muhammad is obviously someone held captive.

Upon thorough review of the life and teachings of Jesus as recorded in the New Testament, there is not a single mention of Jesus ever attending to anyone who was physically being held captive or physically being bruised. A captive is someone that is imprisoned or confined. Bruise means to inflict an injury on someone causing discoloration to the skin. The connotative meaning of bruise in scripture means to hurt, offend, and insult the feelings and social status of another person. Therefore, by intelligent reasoning, the preaching of deliverance to the "captives" and the setting at liberty "those who were bruised" that Jesus spoke of, is obviously referring to the psychological and spiritual captivity of the human person, as well as the diminished value placed upon them from society because of their impoverished social status. The ransoming of "slaves" that Muhammad spoke of was addressing both the setting at liberty those held in physical captivity, as well as setting at liberty those held in psychological and spiritual malaise, from prolonged deprivation of social equality and spiritual progression.

Once again, the teaching of Jesus and Muhammad shows congruence and mutual exchange, sort of an agreeable hand shake of one confirming and corroborating the other. Since it is Muhammad that came nearly 570 years after Jesus, it is Muhammad that is confirming and corroborating the message and teaching of Jesus. It makes sense then, that if Jesus and Muhammad were both prophets sent and missioned by the same One G-d; there would obviously be similar and recurring themes of importance addressed in their message. When Jesus went to the synagogue on the Sabbath day and was presented the book of Esaias to read, he read from a portion that confirmed and corroborated the message of prophet Esaias, and it also validated his own message and teaching. By wisely selecting that portion of the book of prophet Esaias to read from, Jesus showed affiliation and congruence with his own teaching as contained in the Gospel that was given to him.

The message of the Quran given to Muhammad addressed essentially the same matters of social importance addressed by Jesus in the Gospel, and even other critical matters not directly addressed by Jesus; such as the fair and equitable treatment of women and the abhorrent issue of racism, as covered earlier in this book. As mentioned previously, these two major issues became world-wide matters that further exacerbated the moral turpitude of human society. Within the span of approximately 570 years that elapsed between Jesus and Muhammad, these two matters (1) the fair and equitable treatment of women, and (2) the issue of racial and ethnic equality, in addition to the previous mentioned matters of importance, warranted the necessity of "specific address" from G-d to show guidance and liberty where there was tyranny and oppression. The facts are clearly on the table, the proofs are self-evident; Jesus and Muhammad are as 2 Rays shining from The Same Light!

JESUS AND MUHAMMAD ADVOCATED ACTIVE PARTICIPATION FROM THEIR FOLLOWERS

*A*nother aspect that Jesus and Muhammad had in common is that they both conveyed a message of active participation to their followers. Both Jesus and Muhammad urged their followers to be "actively involved" with countering negativity and the undesirable, with positivity and what is good for society. They both knew and understood the consequences that non-engagement and non-involvement from people of faith have; and how this leaves society without a voice of truth to be heard, and without a visual example to serve as a role model. The message of Jesus and Muhammad therefore, challenged each of their followers to be aware of this, and urged them to become beacons of light and hope, in a world where there is much darkness and despair.

In Matthew 5:13-16 of the New Testament, Jesus taught the following:

"You are the salt of the earth, but if salt has lost its savour, wherewith shall it be salted? It is therefore good for nothing, but to be cast out, and trodden under the foot of men. You are the light of the world, a city that is set on a hill cannot be hid. Neither do men light a candle, and put it under a bushel, but on a candlestick; and it gives light unto all that are in the house. Let your light so shine before men that they may see your good works, and glorify your Father which is in heaven."

Jesus refers to his followers as both "salt" and "light", but then says that if the salt has lost its savour (taste), it is good for nothing but to be cast out and trodden under the feet of men. As salt is supposed to enhance, give taste to, and help to preserve foods, Jesus is basically saying his followers should be the same in the society. They are supposed to enhance, give taste (accent), and help preserve the strength and vitality of the human society. By taste in this context, it means they are to enhance society with balance, social good, and pleasant delight that promotes all that is good in society. Jesus also describes his followers as "light", and urges his followers to let their light shine in society so that the world can see their good works. By describing his followers as light for the world, Jesus clearly urges anyone who asserts to be his follower, to be actively involved in "good works" that help bring light to a dark world. He clearly stated, "Neither do men light a candle, and put it under a bushel, but on a candlestick, and it gives light to all that are in the house." In other words, our good works are to be out in the open, not for any gratification or praise, but so that the good works can effect change and become a beacon of light and direction in society.

By tasking his followers with being the "salt of the earth", that implies that there must be social involvement, social responsibility, and moral attention to matters concerning social order. We sprinkle salt over our foods to enhance and give flavor to our dish. If we are to be the salt for the earth, we too must be "sprinkled", that is, we must be directly involved with, and concerned with all social matters that impact human life, for the sake of "enhancing" them with the right seasoning; that is the right stance and moral position.

These words from Jesus about being the salt of the earth and the light for the world, are words tasking anyone who claims to be his follower, to be a person of moral concern, moral action, and having a sense of social obligation to effect change in contemporary society. In other words, these words from Jesus do not allow someone claiming to be his follower, the privilege of sitting quietly on the side line, when situations warrant the need for truths to be spoken, and the correct model to be demonstrated. He is saying, it is not enough for you to just claim to be my follower, you are to prove you are my follower by having the moral courage to be the necessary "salt for the earth and light for the world". In more other words, Jesus was saying, "the earth is always going to need someone who is morally established upon what is true and sound, and willing to stand up against wrong, injustice, unfairness, and all the various sorts of social decadence; I task you therefore, as my followers, to maintain your posture as firm believers in G-d and to be as "salt" for the earth and as "light" for the world, to restore and preserve the best human possibilities, and provide balance and excellent taste (excellent human sensitivity) to all matters of social concern.[1]

The message from Muhammad has a strong resemblance to the message of Jesus. The resemblance is not only obvious, but it further demonstrates that Jesus and Muhammad are as 2 Rays of The Same Light. Remember, Jesus taught his followers to be as "salt for the earth and as light for the world." A look at the message Muhammad taught, conveys essentially the same idea and further emphasizes the point. There are three distinct reference verses in the Quran that Muhammad taught that mirrors the same message of Jesus.

"You are the best of people evolved for mankind, enjoining what is right, forbidding what is wrong, and believing in G-d. If only the People of the Book had faith, it would be best for them: among them are some who do have faith, but most of them are perverted transgressors". Quran 3:110

"Let there arise out of you a band of people inviting to all that is good, enjoining what is right, and forbidding what is wrong: they are the ones to attain felicity". Quran 3:104

"O you who believe! Stand out firmly for justice, as witnesses to G-d, even as against yourselves, or your parents, or your kin, and whether it be against rich or poor: follow not the lusts of your hearts, lest you swerve, and if you distort justice or decline to do justice, verily G-d is well acquainted with all that you do". Quran 4:135

As illustrated in the three verses from the Quran that Muhammad taught, a similar admonishment that was given by Jesus in the New Testament is now being reiterated by Muhammad in the Quran. Not surprisingly, as illustrated in several other previous examples, not only does the message of Muhammad resemble and recapture the "essential idea" Jesus taught, in addition it further expounds on the central theme. For as Jesus taught his followers to be as salt for the earth and as light for the world, Muhammad said, "O you who believe! stand out firmly for justice, as witnesses to G-d, even as against yourselves, or your parents, or your kin, and whether it be against rich or poor. As noted in these verses from the Quran, Muhammad also stated, "let there arise out of you a band of people inviting to all that is good, enjoining what is right, and forbidding what is wrong"; this message is consistent and parallels with Jesus saying "you are the salt of the earth and the light for the world".[2]

The author invites the readers' attention to another similarity in this comparison. When Jesus said that you are the salt of the earth, he further stated, "but if salt has lost its savour, wherewith shall it be salted? It is therefore good for nothing, but to be cast out, and trodden under the foot of men". These words are in fact to be taken as words of caution, not words of caution for the general population, but for those claiming to be his followers but who have become ineffective and of no positive effect for the broader society. He expressed this as salt that has lost its savour. Remember, in this context, Jesus describes the faithful followers as salt, but then says "what good is salt if it has lost its savour. What is this savour? It is its flavor, its ability to "season and enhance", its ability to restore and preserve the best human possibilities and provide balance and excellent taste (excellent human sensitivity) to all matters of social concern. Jesus said but if salt has lost its savour, it is good for nothing but to be trodden under the foot of men. The message of Muhammad from the Quran reiterated the same caution to the faithful followers in similar words, "follow not the lusts of your heart, lest you swerve, and if you distort justice or decline to do justice, verily G-d is well acquainted with all that you do".

It is apparent from the teaching of Jesus in the New Testament and the exhortation of Muhammad from the Quran, both messages are very much parallel to each other, showing much resemblance and congruence. Both Jesus and Muhammad convey a message tasking those who are true believers in G-d, with being actively involved in affecting growth, excellence, and enrichment in the broader society, as well as being actively involved with eradicating all that is against that growth and enrichment. It is also implicit from the verbiage of Jesus in the New Testament and from Muhammad in the Quran, that neither of them condoned a lifestyle of complacency, non-involvement, and inactivity from the people of faith, in the face of decadence, injustice, and bad elements in the broader society. Jesus described the people of faith as being salt of the earth and light for the world, which speaks to their moral and social duty in the community and broader society. The message given to Muhammad in the Quran addressed this same idea by saying "let there arise out of you a band of people inviting to all that is good, enjoining what is right, and forbidding what is wrong", also when it said, "O you who believe! Stand out firmly for justice, as witnesses to G-d, even as against yourselves, or your parents, or your kin, and whether it be against rich or poor: follow not the lusts of your hearts, lest you swerve, and if you distort justice or decline to do justice, verily G-d is well acquainted with all that you do".

Careful review of the words spoken by Jesus and the words spoken by Muhammad indicates once again that their focus and emphasis was from the same perspective. They both were addressing the importance of people of faith affecting change in the community and broader society. They both were reminding the people of faith that by being believers in G-d, you inherit a solemn duty of being actively involved with advocating and promoting what is good and righteous in all facets of human life, as well as the duty of addressing and challenging all the wrong and unjust vices that conflict with the good life G-d intended for the human society. When properly understood, it becomes apparent that Jesus and Muhammad are addressing the same idea, and that is, "what should be the significance of people of faith in relation to the broader society"? By way of a metaphor, Jesus describes the faithful as "salt of the earth" and "light for the world" and describes how they are to impact the society. By way of descriptive language in the Quran, Muhammad describes how the faithful are to be inviting to all that is good, enjoining what is right, forbidding what is wrong, and standing out firmly for justice. Justice is virtually synonymous with balance, and balance as you may recall, is one of the properties of salt.   The message of Jesus and the message of Muhammad therefore, are once again in sync with each other, and as stated earlier in this book, are cut from the same cloth!

JESUS PROMISED THE COMING OF THE COMFORTER, MUHAMMAD IS THE COMFORTER PROMISED BY JESUS

This topic is perhaps one of the most debated discussions amongst fellow worshippers, on the internet, and in published books, concerning differences of opinion in Islam and Christianity. Therefore, first and foremost, the author extends to every reader who may identify themselves as a Christian or Jew, nothing but sincere respect and brotherly love as a believer in G-d and avowed follower of Jesus. As such, this section is not intended to bash or dishonor Christians and Jews, or Christian and Judaic beliefs in anyway, nor is it meant to incite or add to any dissent that may already exist due to differences of opinion. Rather, this section is intended to provide ideas, concepts, and information perhaps not yet familiar to the average reader.

The mention of a "Comforter" being promised by Jesus is mentioned in at least 3 sections in the book of John of the New Testament; John 14: 15-17, John 15: 26-27, and especially John 16: 7-14.

In John 14: 15-17, Jesus says: "If you love me, keep my commandments; and I will pray the Father, and He will give you another Comforter, that he may abide with you forever; Even the Spirit of truth; whom the world cannot receive, because it sees him not neither knows him: but you know him, for he dwells with you, and shall be in you".

In John 15:26-27, Jesus says, "But when the Comforter is come, whom I will send unto you from the Father, even the Spirit of truth, which proceed from the Father, he shall testify of me; And you shall bear witness, because you have been with me from the beginning".

In John 16: 7-14, Jesus says, "Nevertheless I tell you the truth; it is expedient for you that I go away: for if I go not away, the Comforter will not come unto you; but if I depart, I will send him unto you; And when he is come, he will reprove the world of sin, and of righteousness, and of judgement: Of sin, because they believe not on me; of righteousness, because I go unto my Father, and you see me no more; of judgement, because the prince of this world is judged. I have many things to say unto you, but you cannot bear them now; Howbeit when he, the Spirit of Truth is come, he will guide you into all truth: for he shall not speak of himself, but whatsoever he shall hear, that shall he speak: and he will show you things to come. He shall glorify me, for he shall receive of mine, and shall show it unto you".

The author contends that, to understand the correct identity and context of who Jesus was referring to as the "Comforter" that was to come after him, one must put on their thinking cap and carefully examine the scriptures we have just cited, as well as the chronicles of human history. While carefully examining the scriptures, it is important to also consider the denotation and connotation of certain words in scriptural language. For example, there are numerous translations of the New Testament, subsequently one translation may use one word for a description, while another translation may use an entirely different word, for the same object of review. In addition, we must consider the fact that Jesus did not speak English, he primarily spoke Aramaic. Aramaic was the common language spoken in Judea and Jerusalem, as well as the towns Nazareth and Capernaum in Galilee, where Jesus spent much of his time.[1]

It is widely accepted among historians and Biblical scholars alike, that the everyday spoken language of Jesus and his contemporaries, was primarily Aramaic. Although Jesus was obviously familiar with Hebrew and Greek, Aramaic was his primary everyday language spoken. We know Jesus was familiar with Hebrew, because Hebrew was originally the language spoken by the children of Israel, also because Jesus read from the scroll at the synagogue as recorded in Luke 4: 17-18. For Jesus to have read from the scroll, he would have to have known Hebrew. We know that Jesus was also familiar with Greek as well, for in John 18, there is actual dialogue between Jesus and Pontius Pilate, this dialogue would have to have been in Greek. Therefore, Jesus was conveniently familiar with Hebrew and Greek, but Aramaic was primarily his everyday spoken language, as well as the everyday language spoken by his contemporaries. Lastly, we know that Aramaic was the commonly spoken language of Jesus and his disciples because history shows that Aramaic had become the everyday spoken language of the children of Israel, after their forced detention during the Babylonian captivity.[2] As per Matthew 15: 24, Jesus said "I am not sent but unto the lost sheep of the house of Israel". As such, Jesus primarily spoke Aramaic.

Now that we know the language that Jesus primarily spoke was Aramaic, we can now seek to better understand more about the "Comforter" mentioned in the verses we cited earlier. To understand what and who "The Comforter" is, it is essential to go to the source verses where this term is used, but in the language spoken by Jesus, Aramaic. Too much controversy and ambiguity exist concerning this topic of "The Comforter", for us to not go to the source language Jesus spoke, Aramaic. Per the Aramaic New Testament (Peshitta), each time Jesus spoke of "The Comforter", he used the Aramaic term "Paraqlitha". Paraqlitha has been commonly translated into English as Advocate and Comforter.[3]

When the New Testament was being translated from Aramaic into Greek, this Aramaic term Paraqlitha was replaced by the Greek term "Paraclete" which has been translated to mean "Comforter", although other translations also render the terms "Advocate", "Helper", and "Counselor". Christians consider and believe this "Comforter" to be the Holy Spirit, also called Holy Ghost. The author kindly disagrees with this view of the Comforter for several obvious reasons. Per the description of the Comforter as described by Jesus, he had to be describing a flesh and blood person like himself, not the Holy Spirit.

The proof is in John 14: 15-17, Jesus says: "If you love me, keep my commandments; and I will pray the Father, and He will give you another Comforter, that he may abide with you forever; Even the Spirit of truth; whom the world cannot receive, because it sees him not neither knows him: but you know him, for he dwells with you, and shall be in you".

In the above-mentioned verse, Jesus distinctly mentions "another Comforter". The author contends that, by Jesus stating that He will pray the Father and He would give "another Comforter", automatically implies that he himself was a "Comforter" (Advocate and Counselor) type. We all understand the grammatical meaning of the word "another". "Another" refers to an additional person or thing of the same type of something already mentioned or already known about. "Another" can also be used to refer to a different person or thing from the one already known about or mentioned. The first example would be in the statement, "I am unable to teach physics tomorrow, I will inform the front office and they will assign you another teacher in my absence". In this example, it is apparent that the person is a physics teacher, and the front office will assign another "physics teacher" like the one speaking.

The second example would be in the statement, "Next semester, I plan to change my major to another field of study". In this example, someone will be changing their school major to a course of study different from what was previously selected and pursued. In both examples, however, the use of the word "another" implies that the speaker already is or has something of a type, and "another" is coming that may be like or different from what is already in place. Upon further specific inquiry, it was noted that Greek has two words used to define the word "another", (1) *heteros* and (2) *Allos*. When *heteros* is used, it is referring to another, but of a different type and kind. When *Allos* is used, it is referring to another of the same exact type and kind. It just so happens that in the New Testament John 14: 15-17 of the Greek text, *Allos* is used. This means that The Comforter that Jesus was referring to would be someone like himself, a flesh and blood human person, but guided, directed, and inspired by The Holy Spirit. Therefore, the Comforter that Jesus was referring to could not be the Holy Spirit, because the Holy Spirit was already present and with Jesus at his birth, as well as when he went about teaching, preaching, and performing numerous miracles.

There are several verses in the New Testament that repeatedly state that the Holy Spirit was already present and with Jesus; therefore, there was no need of Jesus promising the coming of the Holy Spirit, the Holy Spirit was already present.[4] Please consider the following verses:

Luke 2: 25-29, "And behold, there was a man in Jerusalem whose name was Simeon, and the same man was just and devout, waiting for the consolation of Israel, and the Holy Spirit was upon him; And it was revealed unto him by the Holy Spirit, that he should not see death, before he had seen the Lord's Christ. And he came by the Spirit into the temple: and when the parents bought in the child Jesus, to do for him the custom of the law, then took he him up in his arms, and blessed God, and said, Lord, now let thou thy servant depart in peace according to thy word".

Luke 3: 15-16, "And as the people were in expectation, and all men mused in their hearts of John, whether he was the Christ or not; John answered, saying unto them all, I baptize you with water, but one mightier than I is coming, the latchet of whose shoes I am not worthy to unloose, he shall baptize you with the Holy Spirit and with fire".

Matthew 1:18, "Now the birth of Jesus Christ was on this wise: when as his mother Mary was espoused to Joseph, before they came together, she was found with child of the Holy Spirit".

John 20: 21-23, "Then Jesus said to them again, Peace be unto you: as my Father has sent me, even so I send you; And when he had said this, he breathed on them, and said unto them, "Receive you the Holy Spirit: who so ever sins you remit, they are remitted unto them, and who so ever sins you retain, they are retained".

Luke 4: 18, "The Spirit of the Lord is upon me, because He has anointed me to preach the gospel to the poor, he has sent me to heal the brokenhearted, to preach deliverance to the captives, and recovery of sight to the blind, to set at liberty them that are bruised".

Luke 4: 1, "And Jesus being full of the Holy Spirit returned from Jordan and was led by the Spirit into the wilderness".

As evidenced by the 6 New Testament verses, the Holy Spirit was already present. According to these verses, the Holy Spirit was (1) upon the just and devout man Simeon, (2) the Holy Spirit led Simeon into the temple where he met the child Jesus, (3) the Holy Spirit was upon Jesus and his mother Mary, (4) the Holy Spirit was upon Jesus as he went about preaching and teaching in synagogues, (5) the Holy Spirit was with Jesus as John the Baptist said, Jesus would baptize with the Holy Spirit and with fire, and (6) Jesus was full of the Holy Spirit when he returned from Jordan, and was led into the wilderness.

Therefore, since the Holy Spirit was already present and actively involved with inspiring and guiding Jesus in his preaching, teaching, and many numerous works; it is not plausible, it doesn't make any sense that Jesus would predict the coming of the Holy Spirit, the Holy Spirit was already there! In addition, as further evidence, Jesus would not have said he would pray the Father to send "another Comforter", if he was referring to the Holy Spirit; there is but one Holy Spirit, not two or three!

Also, there is another obvious reason why "The Comforter" Jesus promised to come WAS NOT referring to the "Holy Spirit" as many have misunderstood. Despite the various denominations of present-day Christianity, there are certain theological beliefs and concepts that remain a common thread in every denomination. As such, the Holy Spirit is understood in Christianity to be "The Spirit of G-d", yet having a distinct role and identity, but still part of the trinity concept; Father, Son, and Holy Spirit.

If Father, Son, and Holy Spirit is the perception and concept one may have of G-d, and if you interpret the promised "Comforter" that was to come after Jesus, to be the Holy Spirit; then you are implying that G-d will be interacting with and talking to a part of himself; which is preposterous. According to John 16: 7-14, Jesus stated that it is expedient that he goes away, for if he does not go away the "Comforter" WILL NOT COME. Then, when describing "The Comforter" in verse 13, Jesus stated,

"Howbeit when he the Spirit of Truth is come, he will guide you into all truth: for he shall not speak of himself, but whatsoever he shall hear, that shall he speak: and he will show you things to come".

Ok, let us reason together, since as Jesus said, "The Comforter, the Spirit of Truth", is not going to speak from himself or from his own accord, but that he will be speaking from what he hears; the question naturally follows, who will he be hearing from? Based on logic and what is intelligently sensible in this passage, if you interpret the Comforter, the Spirit of Truth, to be referring to the Holy Spirit; then you are inferring that the Holy Spirit will be hearing from the Father: it is implying that G-d will be speaking to and hearing from himself!! Once again, that concept is preposterous and not sensible! That line of reasoning is absurd, for it suggests that G-d the Father, is going to send his own spirit (the Holy Spirit), and his Holy Spirit is going to hear something from the Father part of himself!! In contemporary psychology, we would call that someone with split personality, multiple personality disorder. Such interpretation and concept for "The Comforter" is not consistent with the majesty and wisdom of G-d!

In addition, Jesus said, he (The Comforter, Spirit of Truth) shall not speak from himself, he shall speak what he hears! Think about it for a moment, that language is not descriptive of the Holy Spirit, that language is descriptive of a human being.

During the research on this subject of The Comforter, the author deemed it necessary to further examine the Greek text again as a qualifying reference. Upon researching the Greek script of the New Testament (John 16: 13) where Jesus describes The Comforter, further proof became obvious that Jesus was referring to an actual person, a flesh and blood human being, who would be sent as The Comforter, and not The Holy Spirit. The Greek script of John 16:13 uses two distinct action verbs describing The Comforter. John 16:13 reads, "Howbeit when he, The Spirit of truth is come, he will guide you into all truth; for he shall not speak from his own accord, but what so ever he shall hear, that shall he speak; and he will show you things to come".

In this passage, the Greek word "hear" is '*akouo*' which means to perceive sound. From this same word '*akouo*', derived the contemporary English word 'acoustics', meaning the study of sound and sound waves. In this same passage, the Greek word to speak is '*laleo*', which casually means 'to emit sounds' and in this specific context it literally means 'to speak'. These two words found in the Greek text of The New Testament are therefore "action verbs", which are describing the physical actions and human functions of "hearing" and "speaking"; which are attributed to a human person who hears something, and then speaks what he heard.

Ok, so think about it, if Jesus was referring to the Holy Spirit coming, he would not have to QUALIFY and VALIDATE the credibility of what he would be speaking, and what he would be hearing! The Holy Spirit needs no validation, never did, and never will! The Holy Spirit is the divine spirit of G-d that guides, inspires, and teaches those chosen by G-d, for His select purpose. Jesus was not qualifying and validating the Holy Spirit, Jesus was qualifying and validating a human person who would be inspired and guided by the Holy Spirit; for the express purpose of speaking and guiding others into truths that Jesus himself pointed to. It is the person that G-d selected and inspired through the Holy Spirit, that would speak exactly what he heard!

Once again, carefully consider the words and context of the following reference verses:

In John 14: 15-17, Jesus says: "If you love me, keep my commandments; and I will pray the Father, and He will give you another Comforter, that he may abide with you forever; Even the Spirit of truth; whom the world cannot receive, because it sees him not neither knows him: but you know him, for he dwells with you, and shall be in you".

In John 15:26-27, Jesus says, "But when the Comforter is come, whom I will send unto you from the Father, even the <u>Spirit of truth</u>, which proceed from the Father, he shall testify of me; And you shall bear witness, because you have been with me from the beginning".

In John 16: 7-14, Jesus says, "Nevertheless I tell you the truth; it is expedient for you that I go away: for if I go not away, the Comforter will not come unto you; but if I depart, I will send him unto you; And when he is come, he will reprove the world of sin, and of righteousness, and of judgement: Of sin, because they believe not on me; of righteousness, because I go unto my Father, and you see me no more; of judgement, because the prince of this world is judged. I have many things to say unto you, but you cannot bear them now; Howbeit when he, the <u>Spirit of Truth</u> is come, he will guide you into all truth: for he shall not speak of himself, but whatsoever he shall hear, that shall he speak: and he will show you things to come. He shall glorify me, for he shall receive of mine, and shall show it unto you".

According to John 16: 7-14, Jesus said it is expedient that he goes away, for if he does not go away, "The Comforter" WILL NOT come. He didn't say The Comforter probably would not come, or more than likely would not come; Jesus specifically said THE COMFORTER WILL NOT COME, until and unless he goes away! Therefore, by reasoning of Jesus own words, The Comforter that was to come COULD NOT be referring to the Holy Spirit, the Holy Spirit was already there; Jesus was already filled with the Holy Spirit! Therefore, since The Comforter that was to come was not referring to the Holy Spirit, who then was this referring to?

As we identify and explore this answer, please remember the author in no way seeks to discredit or dishonor the noble beliefs and stature of the Christian or Judaic faith, rather, the sole purpose is to further demonstrate once again, that Jesus and Muhammad are indeed 2 Rays of The Same Light!

We have reviewed and demonstrated how and why "The Comforter" that was to come COULD NOT be the Holy Spirit. As we have clearly shown that the Holy Spirit was already there and very much present in the life and works of Jesus. Despite this elucidation, for those perhaps not yet convinced and still think "The Comforter" that was to come is referring to the Holy Spirit; please consider once again the final reference verse uttered by Jesus.

In John 16: 7-14, Jesus says, "Nevertheless I tell you the truth; it is expedient for you that I go away: for if I go not away, the Comforter will not come unto you; but if I depart, I will send him unto you; And when he is come, he will reprove the world of sin, and of righteousness, and of judgement: Of sin, because they believe not on me; of righteousness, because I go unto my Father, and you see me no more; of judgement, because the prince of this world is judged. I have many things to say unto you, but you cannot bear them now; Howbeit when he, the <u>Spirit of Truth</u> is come, he will guide you into all truth: for he shall not speak of himself, but whatsoever he shall hear, that shall he speak: and he will show you things to come. He shall glorify me, for he shall receive of mine, and shall show it unto you".

In the above verse, as well as in two of our other reference verses cited from John of the New Testament, Jesus gives a "helpful hint" and "distinguishing clue" of, (1) who "The Comforter" is, (2) what will happen when he comes, and (3) how this would come about. Jesus gave this hint and clue by adding another complimentary "nick name and alias name" to The Comforter; Jesus refers to The Comforter as the "Spirit of Truth".

Jesus was very much aware of the ambiguity and controversy that would develop concerning "The Comforter", also referred to as "The Spirit of Truth", that was to come after him. Jesus knew this, just as he knew that many were already ambiguous and questionable about his own role and mission as the awaited "messiah". Biblical historians and Christian scholars affirm that the Jewish leadership during the time of Jesus, had a much different idea and perception about the "messiah" that was to come. They were anticipating someone who would be "The King of the Jews", an earthly king and ruler type, someone who would liberate them from the oppressive Roman constraints. The New Testament further indicates, and history records that King Herod ruled Judea under the Romans, and therefore felt "threatened" of this awaited messiah, Jesus. Jesus however did not come preaching and teaching the kingdom of Israel per se, Jesus came teaching the kingdom of G-d! As mentioned previously, despite Jesus clearly stating that, "I am not sent but unto the lost sheep of the house of Israel" (Matthew 15:24), it was this same "lost sheep", particularly the religious leadership, who misunderstood and dishonored Jesus in their own synagogues and temples. Not surprisingly, when Jesus gave prophecy that a "Comforter" would come after him, someone he also referred to as the "Spirit of Truth", once again he was misunderstood by the same "lost sheep".[5]

According to John 16: 13-14, Jesus said:

"Nevertheless I tell you the truth; it is expedient for that I go away: for if I go not away, the Comforter will not come unto you; but if I depart, I will send him unto you; And when he is come, he will reprove the world of sin, and of righteousness, and of judgement: Of sin, because they believe not on me; of righteousness, because I go unto my Father, and you see me no more; of judgement, because the prince of this world is judged. I have many things to say unto you, but you cannot bear them now; Howbeit when he, the Spirit of Truth is come, he will guide you into all truth: for he shall not speak of himself, but whatsoever he shall hear, that shall he speak: and he will show you things to come. He shall glorify me, for he shall receive of mine, and shall show it unto you".

According to these verses, Jesus said there are MANY things he would like to have said and explored, but he said to the people, "you cannot bare them now", in other words; they were not ready, the time had not come.

I am quite sure that Jesus would like to have addressed such critical subjects as (1) the nature and status of women in society, the fair and equitable treatment they are due, their civic rights and equal entitlements like that of men, the respect and regard they are due as mothers and first educators of children, etc. and (2) the issue of racism and ethnic equality, with the inferiority and superiority complexes that divides man from man, having one race of people perceive themselves as being superior to another race based on color and ethnicity; which by the way happens to be perhaps one of the most critical issues of our country and the world at large!

These are but 2 of several other major social issues that Jesus was alluding to when he said, "there are MANY things I would like to say to you, but you cannot bare them now! Interestingly, it is these 2 major issues, (1) the nature and status of women in society, to include their civic rights and equal entitlements and (2) the issue of racism, with the inferiority and superiority complexes in certain races and ethnic groups, that has not only divided man from man along lines of color and ethnicity, but for many years continued to influence biased politics affecting the status of social equality. As recently stated, these 2 critical issues became perhaps the 2 most formidable matters on the table of world politics and American history. Not surprisingly, Jesus said "The Comforter, The Spirit of Truth", that was to come after him, he would address these matters and guide the people into all truth!

In previous chapters, as we compared the sermons of Jesus and Muhammad delivered from the location of a mountain, we demonstrated and provided undebatable, historical evidence of Muhammad addressing these and other critical issues in his last sermon and farewell address on Mount Arafat. In summation, as it pertains to The Comforter and Spirit of Truth foretold by Jesus, we have deliberated and elucidated much already, on how this COULD NOT and WAS NOT referring to the Holy Spirit. With humility and assurance, the author contends that Muhammad is that Comforter, and that Muhammad is the "Spirit of Truth" Jesus was referring to!

MUHAMMAD: THE COMFORTER, THE SPIRIT OF TRUTH

*A*s mentioned at the beginning of this book, the author humbly asks each reader to utilize two valuable assets in the pages to follow; they are the gifts of (1) **unbiased inductive observation** and (2) **sound deductive reasoning**. It is important that your observation continue to be unbiased, so that introduced facts about Muhammad are not at odds and possibly competing with previous "biased views or arbitrary notions" not supported by the authentic pages of history. As well, it is equally important that your deductive reasoning continue to be sound, and that your analysis and conclusions remain consistent with evidence substantiated by history and "common sense"; although this "sense" may not be common among those not correctly informed about Muhammad. Due to an abundance of misinformation on the biographical subject of Muhammad, blatant alteration and/or exaggeration of known historical accounts, the author is very much aware of the complexity that this presents to the novice reader. Respectfully therefore, a suggested reading list is presented at the end of this book for further review and research.

To adequately address the subject of Muhammad being "The Comforter and Spirit of Truth" that Jesus was referring to in the New Testament, it is essential and necessary to also briefly discuss the subject of the Quran; for this is the message and teaching from G-d that Muhammad subsequently taught and lived by. As we briefly explore a few historical facts about Muhammad and the Quran, the objective is to (1) provide pertinent information with those who may not be adequately informed, (2) identify and clarify inaccurate heresy, and (3) address common misconceptions. With this objective in mind the author aims at, once again illustrating our central theme, that Jesus and Muhamad are as 2 Rays of The Same Light!

MUHAMMAD: A BRIEF HISTORICAL SKETCH

A full and inclusive biography of Muhammad is not absolutely required here. However, the author deems it necessary to at least present a brief sketch of Muhammad, as well as a concise review of the message that gave impetus to his mission, the Quran. In this brief synopsis, our main concentration are those details and facts about Muhammad that (1) are confirmed and can be corroborated by historical review, (2) demonstrate and intelligently establish the validity of Muhammad as being "The Comforter and Spirit of Truth" mentioned by Jesus in the New Testament, and (3) illustrate and convincingly prove that the Quran is not only the revelation from G-d that empowered and inspired Muhammad, but also that the Quran is "the very message" that Jesus was referring to when he said, "The Comforter shall only speak what he hears, and not from his own accord".

Muhammad was born nearly 570 years after Jesus, in Mecca, Arabia. His father, Abdullah, died before he was born, and his mother, Amina, died when he was just six years old. He was subsequently cared for by his paternal grandfather, Abd al Muttalib for only two years, at which time he also passed away.[1]

Now eight years old, Muhammad began to live with his uncle, Abu Talib. As a young child living with his uncle, Muhammad learned the chores of a shepherd, and as a young teen his interests and favorable circumstances afforded him the opportunity to work as a young merchant, accompanying his uncle. During this time, Mecca was considered a highly significant pilgrimage center, and as well, Mecca was favorably located and therefore connected to many of the caravan trade routes to such places as Syria, Egypt, and even Yemen. As a young merchant in Mecca, as well as on caravan routes to trade centers with his uncle, Muhammad was found to be highly resourceful, and his prestige and likeability spread far and wide. Untainted by the propensities of youth, and despite having been an orphan since age six, Muhammad excelled tremendously in having an abundance of social attributes and inherent personal values.[2]

The excellent social attributes of Muhammad were quite impressionable upon all who encountered him as a young merchant. His inherent personal values, even as a youth, made him stand out head-and-shoulders amongst his peers. His honorable reputation and stature as a fair and equitable merchant in business dealings, and his everyday normal interactions with people in Mecca were of such high character, that people began calling him by two distinct nick names. Historians report that Muhammad was soon being called "El Amin" by many, and others also would call him "El Sadeeq".[3]

Although his name was rightfully Muhammad, people began calling him these two nick names, El Amin and El Sadeeq. "El Amin" refers to someone who has a reputation for being trustworthy, reliable, and dependable. "El Sadeeq" refers to someone who has a reputation for being honest, sincere, and truthful. While diligently researching the profile of Muhammad from several sources, the author found it interesting that in virtually every source narrating Muhammad's early life in Mecca, historians and religious scholars alike, some who obviously did not agree with his religious position; yet their biographies report that the people of Mecca used to call Muhammad by these two distinct nick names, "El Amin (The Trustworthy and Dependable) and also "El Sadeeq" (The Honest and Truthful). It is reported that Muhammad had become so well known in Mecca as El Amin and El Sadeeq, that many years later when he began to openly denounce the pagan customs and beliefs of Arabia, even his enemies often referred to him as El Amin and El Sadeeq!

Now 25 years old, as fate would have it, the qualities and sobriquet of Muhammad as "El Amin" (The Trustworthy and Dependable) and "El Sadeeq" (The Truthful and Honest) had become so well known, that he was inquired about and soon employed by a wealthy merchant by the name of Khadijah. Khadijah, age 40, was a wealthy business woman in Mecca who used to employ experienced merchants to manage her merchandise on various caravan expeditions. After hearing much admirable reputation and commendable reviews about "El Amin and El Sadeeq", Khadijah offered Muhammad an opportunity to work as her agent on a highly anticipated trade expedition to Syria. Muhammad gladly accepted her offer and made preparation to head to Syria. This expedition was indeed monumental and quite profitable for Muhammad. Upon his return to Mecca, Khadijah was highly pleased and truly amazed at the merchandise acquisition and monetary profit Muhammad managed to secure. As such, Khadijah was so impressed with the integrity, trustworthiness, and business acumen of Muhammad; she not only put Muhammad in charge of other future business endeavors, she asked for his hand in marriage; and Muhammad graciously accepted her proposal!

So it was, Khadijah was 40 years old and Muhammad was 25, yet their marital relationship was one of mutual respect, honor, and love. They were married at least 15 years before history, unlike anything Khadijah or Muhammad ever imagined or expected, would begin to unfold for Muhammad.   During the next 15 years, the popularity and credibility of Muhammad as El Amin (The Trustworthy) and El Sadeeq (The Truthful and Honest) continued to resonate among the people of Mecca. Muhammad however, was clearly not a product of the thinking and life style of Arabia, and especially not a product of the mind set and status quo in Mecca. From the time as an orphaned child, on to becoming a young adult, Muhammad always showed much dislike and aversion to the uncouth and benighted ways of Mecca.[4]

As you may know, Arabia during this time in history, was referred to as "Jahiliyyah" by religious historians. The term "Jahiliyyah" means "the period of Ignorance". While there were obviously other parts of the world that had degrees of immorality, social darkness, turmoil, and lawlessness; Arabia by far, was the lowest of the low. Arabia, to especially include Mecca, looked something like this. Though there were some Christians and Jews present, there numbers and moral impact was inconsequential, subsequently they posed no major social affect or influence on the greater society. Paganism and idolatry were the order of the day. Arabs practiced extreme idol worship. There was a g-d for this, a g-d for that; a g-ddess for this and a g-ddess for that. Idols of all shapes and sizes were revered and believed to have power over their fate. They were also highly submerged in the superstitious belief in omens, astrology, soothsaying, and even seeking blessings from certain objects. Social disorder and anarchy were also the order of the day, with the complete absence of any form of government; thereby allowing the absolute freedom of the individual to do as one willed without any moral constraints.

The only authority recognized by the Arabs was the authority of tribal chiefs. Therefore, tribalism was the way of life, and it was a life of pandemonium and absolute mayhem. There was no such thing as what we now call, "basic human rights", that idea was non-existent. There was no sense of shame, and no matter how uncouth or uncivilized something may have appeared, nothing at all was considered inappropriate. Gambling and compulsive drunkenness was another iniquity among the Arabs, so much so, intoxication was considered the norm and sobriety was considered abnormal.

Women had no rights or social status and were considered nothing more than mere sex objects.[5] Not only was adultery rampant in their society, but among the Arabs it had also become acceptable for a step son to marry his step-mother, or even a brother to marry his own sister. One of the most ignorant and heinous customs of the Arabs also during this time was the killing of their female children. This barbaric custom of killing their female children was done for three abhorrent reasons, (1) as a sacrifice to some of their idol gods hoping to please them, (2) out of fear of poverty, and (3) the over dose of male chauvinism was such that, the birth of a female child was considered a moment of immense shame and embarrassment, and newborn female infants were often buried alive to avoid this sense of disgrace and social humiliation.[6]

This is only a brief and condensed snap shot of what Arabia was like many years before, and during the early years of Muhammad. As mentioned earlier, a full and inclusive biography of Muhammad is not absolutely required or possible here due to space, however a concise summary was necessary to lay the desired foundation. As such, now married at age 25, to his wife Khadijah age 40, the next 15 years for Muhammad proved to be a period of observation, reflection, and ultimately the unfolding of history and fulfillment of prophecy.[7]

For the next 15 years, the "Jahiliyyah" Period of Ignorance throughout Arabia, and particularly Mecca, began having a more compelling impact upon the mind and spirit of Muhammad. Despite the pagan idolatrous beliefs and uncivilized Arab customs that were rampant in Mecca, with all the unthinkable and inhumane acts of cruelty, anarchy, and immorality that was considered normal; Muhammad was never drawn to, condoned, or participated in such acts or customs in the least. On the contrary, Muhammad seemed always aloof and avoidant of the pagan idolatrous beliefs and uncouth lifestyle of Mecca. You would perhaps think that a child orphaned at an early age, having lost his father before or at birth, having lost his mother by age six, and then a dear grandfather by age 8; you would perhaps consider such person more predisposed to being emotionally or socially unstable. Quite the opposite, Muhammad not only had a stable and well-protected, well-balanced emotional development as a young adult, he also possessed an array of noble human qualities. His proclivity for trustworthiness, rectitude, and integrity were   such that earned him the nick names, El Amin (The Trustworthy) and El Sadeeq (The Truthful and Honest).[8]

Yet, despite Muhammad's growing reputation for nobility and excellent character that distinguished him from his contemporaries, he eventually found himself from time to time withdrawing to a remote place, a cave called Hira, to have a brief period of solitude away from the idolatrous and uncouth lifestyle of Mecca. Historians report that Muhammad often went to this cave during the month of Ramadan for brief retreat.

Muhammad went to this cave seeking an opportunity to think, contemplate, and to find some sense of inner peace away from the chaos and social darkness of Mecca. He felt a heavy weight upon him, for in his soul and conscience, he knew that what he saw in Mecca could not be the way things were meant to be. He knew that the idols people revered and prayed to in Mecca were not deserving of worship or adoration. He knew, despite having lost his mother at age six, that women were not meant to be treated unfairly, nor meant to be treated as mere sex objects as they were. He felt much discontent and indignation each time he learned the news of another female infant that had been buried alive. He was overly perplexed by the habitual drunkenness he saw and chaotic tribalism that kept various tribes constantly warring with each other.

Muhammad, now age 40, had come to the cave Hira on other similar occasions; primarily to think, fast, and search within his soul for answers and solutions to all the immoral practices, idolatrous beliefs, inhumane social customs, and the seemingly complete loss of spiritual direction in Arabian society. Again, Muhammad had come other times to this cave seeking solitude to search within his soul, to cry out to the universe, fasting, trying to find a balance between all the decadence that surrounded him; versus the sense of purity in his own heart and soul for what he perceived to be true and right. Interestingly, on one specific night while Muhammad was in this cave, something happened that had never happened before. It was truly a life changing moment, one that completely overwhelmed Muhammad with intense mystery and enigma; and a moment that would begin to change the course of human history.

One remarkable night while Muhammad was in the cave, heavily engaged in fervent contemplation and intense soul searching, he received a very strange and unannounced visit! This visit was tremendously extraordinary, tremendously extraordinary because only select, carefully chosen individuals in history have ever received a visit of this profound magnitude, and from this exclusive visitor.

The exclusive visitor that came to Muhammad was none other than the distinguished angel, Gabriel.[9] Biblical and other religious scholars describe the angel Gabriel as the messenger-agent, whose primary role and responsibility is to convey and deliver specific messages directly from G-d. As the messenger agent of G-d, Gabriel is distinctly mentioned at least 4 times in the Bible, (1) Daniel 8:16 and Daniel 9:21 with the prophet Daniel, (2) Luke 1:19 with Zachariah, and (3) Luke 1:26 with Mary, the mother of Jesus. Interestingly, in each of these encounters where Gabriel appears before Daniel, Zachariah, and Mary, each of them initially experienced exactly what Muhammad experienced, an immediate sense of fear!

Like the Biblical accounts of Mary, Zachariah, and especially Daniel (Daniel 8:16-17) upon being approached by the angel Gabriel; Muhammad also felt a stunning sense of fear, as the angel Gabriel approached him closer and said "Iqraa" (Read and Recite). Muhammad, still with a sense of fear and panic, responded to the angel Gabriel by saying, "I cannot read or recite". Then it is reported that the angel Gabriel embraced him tightly, and upon releasing him he said again to Muhammad, "Iqraa" (Read and Recite), to which Muhammad replied again, "I cannot read or recite". Again, Gabriel embraced Muhammad tightly saying, "Iqraa" (Read and Recite), Muhammad again responded by saying, "I cannot read or recite".

For the third time, Gabriel embraced Muhammad squeezing him tightly, and upon releasing him, Gabriel said,

"Read and Recite, in the Name of Your Lord and Cherisher who created, created man from a germ cell that clings (alaq), Read and Recite, for your Lord is Most Bountiful and Generous, He who has taught by the pen, taught man what he was before not knowing".

Upon hearing these words from the angel Gabriel, Muhammad repeated back to him exactly what he heard, word for word. Immediately thereafter, Gabriel quickly departed, and Muhammad, now trembling with fear, overwhelmed with suspense and anxiety, hurried home to his wife Khadijah and informed her of what had just took place in the cave. Still very much overwhelmed by the complexity of events, Khadijah tried best as possible to allay Muhammad's fears and anxieties. When Muhammad related to her the details of what he saw and exactly what he heard, she decided to consult a reliable and knowledgeable resource, her cousin Waraqah. Waraqah was a learned Christian who was very familiar with the narratives of other individuals in scripture such as Zachariah, Mary the mother of Jesus, and Daniel, all of whom had similar experiences upon being approached by the angel Gabriel, as that described now by Muhammad. Waraqah was quite familiar with the New Testament teachings of Jesus, to include the prophecy of Jesus describing the coming of the "Comforter and Spirit of Truth" who was to come after him. Waraqah was especially familiar with the description that Jesus gave of "The Comforter", as one who would "speak whatsoever he hears, and not from his own accord". Upon learning the details of what happened in the cave with Muhammad and what was said to him, Waraqah informed Muhammad that what he experienced in the cave was not a figment of his imagination, nor was he possessed or anything of the sort. He told Muhammad that he had just been visited by the angel Gabriel, and that he had just been chosen as the prophet of G-d for a select purpose. He further warned Muhammad that "the majority in Mecca will begin to call you a liar, they will begin to mistreat you, they will attempt to cast you out and eventually they will make war upon you; for a prophet was always without honor in his own country". [10]

So it was, this was the beginning of events for Muhammad being visited by the angel Gabriel in a manner quite similar to that mentioned in the Bible of Zachariah, Mary the mother of Jesus, and Daniel; for the express purpose of receiving a specific message from G-d. For the next 23 years, at different intervals of time and location, Muhammad would continue to receive revelations from G-d by way of the angel Gabriel. The actual size of the messages would usually vary, sometimes short succinct verses, and other times, lengthy passages.

The subject matter of these revelations were very comprehensive and truly diverse, comprised of numerous passages addressing a myriad of pertinent social matters, chronicles of previous prophets, words of glorification and praise due to G-d, ethical virtues and moral standards for the individual and society, reminders of man having proper regard and fear of displeasing G-d, the fair and equitable treatment of women, the vital subject of "racial equality", and the parity due to all ethnic groups inhabiting the earth, reminders of man having honor and high regard for parents and extended family ties, reminders of the Judgement Day and that we all must account to G-d for all of our actions; also profound narrations of phenomena in creation and scientific observations that were only to be discovered and affirmed many years later after the Quran was revealed. All this and so much more was conveyed to Muhammad by way of the angel Gabriel and is commonly known as the Quran.

There is much that can be said of how the people of Mecca, and Arabia at large, began to respond to the message, as Muhammad began to "speak what he heard", by way of the angel Gabriel. However, our central theme and purpose here is to illustrate that what Muhammad heard by way of the angel Gabriel, is in fact what Jesus was referring to when he said,

In John 16: 7-14, Jesus says, "Nevertheless I tell you the truth; it is expedient for you that I go away: for if I go not away, the Comforter will not come unto you; but if I depart, I will send him unto you; And when he is come, he will reprove the world of sin, and of righteousness, and of judgement: Of sin, because they believe not on me; of righteousness, because I go unto my Father, and you see me no more; of judgement, because the prince of this world is judged. I have many things to say unto you, but you cannot bear them now; Howbeit when he, the <u>Spirit of Truth</u> is come, he will guide you into all truth: for he shall not speak from himself, but whatsoever he shall hear, that shall he speak: and he will show you things to come. He shall glorify me, for he shall receive of mine, and shall show it unto you".

Upon detailed inspection, unbiased review, and principle-to-principle comparative study of the teachings of both Jesus and Muhammad, the author is convinced that Muhammad is the one Jesus was referring to. As I compared the message of what Muhammad taught, and that message being exactly what he heard; and then compared that to the message of what Jesus taught, it was easy to connect the dots and see the continuity of truth and fulfillment of promise.

In the prediction Jesus gave about The Comforter, there are 3 distinct things he stated that would be a part of his distinguished resume. Jesus said that when The Comforter comes, he would (1) reprove the world of sin, (2) reprove the world of righteousness, and (3) reprove the world of judgement. With a brief snap shot, we have just painted a vivid picture of the promiscuous sin, indiscriminate unrighteousness, and complete absence of sound judgement, called "Jahiliyyah"; that profiled the people of Mecca, and Arabia at large.

Reprove means to reprimand, to rebuke, to chastise, and to admonish; and with the message that Muhammad received, that is exactly what he did! Muhammad not only began to rebuke and reprimand the people of Mecca for their sin, unrighteousness, and absence of sound judgement; but the message he was given also served as a moral and educational admonishment towards what they should be. Hence, it is one thing to chastise and reprimand someone for their sin, unrighteousness, and absence of good judgement; it is another thing to go the extra step by educating and demonstrating by example, what is the right way. Again, this is exactly what Muhammad did.

The sins that Muhammad rebuked pertaining to worship included (1) the sin of believing in and worshipping idols and any graven images as G-d,[11] (2) the sin of associating partners or any other associates with G-d, (3) the sin of attributing divinity and holiness to anyone other than G-d (4) the sin of hypocrisy, where we say we believe in G-d, but knowingly either do the things that G-d has forbidden, or the sin of consistently failing to do the things G-d has said we are supposed to do, (4) the sin of pretentious worship, where we put on an ostentatious show and superficial public display of worship, in order to impress others and win favor, but not really having a sincere motive and desire to please G-d.

As it pertains to the subject of righteousness, Muhammad rebuked the concept of righteousness, [12] as described in this passage from the Quran; chapter 2 verse 177:

"It is not righteousness that you turn your faces towards East or West; but it is righteousness to believe in Allah(G-d) and the Last Day, and the Angels, and the Scriptures, and the Messengers, and to spend out of your substance and out of love for Him(G-d), for your kin, for the orphans, for the needy, for the wayfarer, for those who ask, and for the ransom of slaves; to be steadfast in prayer, and practice regular charity; to fulfill the contracts which you have made, and to be firm and patient in pain or suffering and adversity; and throughout all periods of panic. Such are the people of truth, the G-d-fearing"!

Righteousness also rebuked in Quran; 17: 23-26

Your Lord has decreed that you worship none but Him, and that you be kind to your parents; whether one or both of them attain old age in your life, say not to them a word of contempt, nor repel them, but address them in terms of honor; and out of kindness, lower to them the wing of humility, and say: "O my Lord, bestow on them Your Mercy even as they cherished me in childhood"; Your Lord knows best what is in your hearts: if you do deeds of righteousness, verily He is Most Forgiving to those who turn to Him again and again in true penitence; And render to your kindred their due rights, and also to those in need, and to the wayfarer: but squander not your wealth in the manner of a spendthrift.

Jesus also said "The Comforter" would reprove the world of judgement![13] During my review of the teachings of Muhammad from the context of judgement, I noticed that among the other relevant matters that he addressed, there were 2 specific critical issues that Muhammad reproved and gave exclusive attention to! By the way, these 2 critical issues are of such volatile nature, they inevitably became perhaps the two most pressing issues that challenged the moral and ethical fiber of every society. These 2 critical issues that Muhammad reproved and gave exclusive attention to were (1) the subject of racism and ethnic equality in society, and (2) the fair, kind, and equitable treatment of women; to include their civic entitlements and their equal status in society.

As previously illustrated, Muhammad adequately addressed these two delicate, but critical issues in his Last Sermon from Mount Arafat.

The region and era of Jesus had two things in common with the era of Muhammad. Those two things were (1) the low perception and inferior status of women, and (2) the existence of social inequalities and privileges based on the status of race, ethnicity, and social class. If you were to search the New Testament accounts of Matthew, Mark, Luke, and John, line for line, page to page, you will not find any mention of Jesus explicitly addressing or admonishing the critical subjects of racism, racial and ethnic equality, inferiority and superiority complexes among racial groups, or the favoritism, bias, and inequalities in society based on ethnicity and race. Nor will you find any words in the New Testament from Jesus explicitly addressing or advocating the need for fair, equitable, and kind treatment of women, to include their due right to domestic and civic respect, and equal entitlement.

These observations are not intended to imply that Jesus overlooked, forgot, or fell short in anyway. Nor is it meant, with any bias or favoritism, to over-exaggerate and credit Muhammad with having said or done something that Jesus didn't say or do! Let us not forget Jesus own words, he said "THERE ARE MANY THINGS I WOULD LIKE TO SAY UNTO YOU, but you cannot bear them now, however when He, The Spirit of Truth is come, HE will guide you into all truth, for He will not speak from His own accord, but shall speak what so ever He hears". Therefore, by his own literal words and by intelligent inference from his literal words, Jesus was saying that the Spirit of Truth, The Comforter, when He comes, He will address, expound on, and advocate these pertinent and critical issues and many other things that I would like to address; but you cannot bear them now!

In summary, these observations are but a few of the critical issues and insights that Jesus was referring to in the New Testament when he said, "I have many things to say unto you, but you cannot bear them now. However, when He, The Spirit of Truth is come, he will guide you into all truth: for he will not speak from his own accord, but what so ever he hears, that shall he speak, and he will show you things to come" (John 16: 12-13).

With humility, yet also with assurance acquired from close inspection, side-by-side comparison, and unbiased reasoning, the author once again contends that the one Jesus was referring to who would come after him, is none other than Muhammad. Because of his genuine proclivity for trustworthiness, honesty, and excellence of character, despite the ignorant, uncivilized, and uncouth lifestyle of Mecca, Muhammad became commonly known as EL Sadeeq (The Truthful and Honest) and EL Amin (The Trustworthy), and this was long before he began receiving any revelations by way of the angel Gabriel.

The author considers it highly significant and a clue for those who ponder, that Jesus referred to the promised Comforter as "The Spirit of Truth", and that Muhammad even as a young adult, had such a chaste and honorable reputation as someone who lived by the "Spirit of Truth"; so much so, that the people from his own city bestowed upon him the nickname of "The Trustworthy" (EL Amin) and (El Sadeeq) "The Honest One" long before the events of Gabriel conveying the messages of the Quran. Thereafter, this same one who they referred to as The Trustworthy and Honest One, suddenly receives a message from G-d that, as Jesus said, would reprove the world of sin, righteousness, and judgement.

As illustrated in several topics discussed throughout this book, the message given to Muhammad repeatedly affirmed, endorsed, further expounded on, and gave broader meaning and demonstration of the message and teaching of Jesus.

Contrary to the popular misconceptions among those not correctly informed, the teachings of Jesus and Muhammad are not only complementary and relative to each other; but when properly understood, they fit together like pieces of a composite whole. In our incredible information age, where data is readily available to everyone by the click of a button on our phones and laptops, the use of critical thinking becomes highly imperative to discern what is sensible, consistent, and clear; from that which is irrational, inconsistent, and ambiguous. Amid the numerous selections of biased reports and disingenuous comparisons of Jesus and Muhammad on the publication market, the hope of this book was to encourage each person to think outside the box of the status quo. The object was to open another vista, another view and panorama, in hopes of showing something perhaps never viewed before; that Jesus and Muhammad are as 2 Rays of the Same Light!

The author has deliberated much about Jesus and Muhammad being as 2 Rays of the Same Light. A variety of subjects have been explored where we have clearly shown the similarity and consistency in the messages taught by Jesus and Muhammad. An in-depth analogy and examination were done, where we intelligently concluded that the promised one foretold by Jesus, could not be referring to the Holy Spirit. We illustrated by several examples from the New Testament that the Holy Spirit was already present. Subsequently, during the presentation and discussion of Muhammad being the Comforter and Spirit of Truth foretold by Jesus, we identified the Quran as being "the message" that Muhammad heard, over a span of 23 years, by way of the angel Gabriel. Aware of possible reservations, doubts, and uncertainties some people may have regarding the authenticity and legitimacy of the Quran, the author has prepared an illustration of examples that serve as undebatable evidence, food for thought, and proof of the Quran's source and origin.

THE QURAN: THE MESSAGE "HEARD" BY MUHAMMAD

The average reader has either read or at least heard of some of the profound miracles that are attributed to Jesus in the New Testament. With each of these profound miracles performed by Jesus, he humbly credits G-d as "The One" who granted him the power and ability to do what he did. In other words, it wasn't from any innate powers or inherent abilities that Jesus himself possessed, it was from the unimaginable majestic power and sublime wisdom from G-d, bestowed upon Jesus, which gave him such abilities to do great and marvelous works.[1] None the less, these miracles were truly astonishing and quite profound to say the least. Miraculous powers on different levels of human affect, was bestowed from G-d upon several prophets at distinct times to inspire faith in the people, to give an idea of the unimaginable power of G-d to do what so ever He wills, and to warn sinners and unbelievers of the price of disobedience. Interestingly, in the category of comparing miracles performed by Jesus and miracles attributed to Muhammad, the evidence takes on a different weight.

The great miracle granted to Muhammad was of a different magnitude and proportion than that granted to Jesus. The great miracle given to Muhammad was in the form of a weighty message (The Quran), a message that would among other things, recapture and reiterate much of what was conveyed to the prophets and messengers before, and so much more.

The "miraculous gift" in this weighty message was it containing exact descriptions about numerous scientific phenomena that was only to be discovered and/or intelligently explained several hundred years after Muhammad. This same miracle, in the form of knowledge, would later enhance the dawning of enlightenment in many branches of science that would impact the world.

As we read about the numerous miracles performed by Jesus in the New Testament, we have no other option but to humbly acknowledge and accept the undeniable power of G-d working through Jesus. In like manner, as we explore some of the scientific expositions that were revealed to Muhammad in the Quran, that were not known at that time; we have no other option but to humbly acknowledge and once again accept the undeniable power of G-d, this time working through Muhammad!

The author contends that G-d, who is All Knowing, already knew that there would be some doubts, hesitations, and ambiguity with respect to the message given to Muhammad (The Quran). The author further contends that G-d is also All Wise, which means that not only does G-d know absolutely everything, but He also perfectly knows and understands the cause and effect, the before and the after, the apparent and that which is hidden, and especially the beginning and the culmination of all events.

Upon this premise, the author asserts that G-d specifically imparted knowledge to Muhammad of certain natural and scientific phenomenon that was not known at the time, and gave him the exact description and sequence of certain occurrences, as an affirmation and eternal proof that the message of the Quran could only be from one source, G-d, The Creator Supreme, The All Knowing, The All Wise, Lord of all worlds and systems of knowledge.[2]

As we explore some of these "proofs" that were revealed to Muhammad in the Quran, it is important for each reader to remember that at the time that these things were revealed to Muhammad, the intricate knowledge of such had not been discovered, advocated, or proven anywhere, and was therefore not known. There were no intelligent or coherent explanations amongst those regarded as "learned in science", capable of accurately explaining such things as they were explained when the Quran was revealed to Muhammad.

Subsequently, it was not until after the Quran was revealed to Muhammad, many years after, that scientific inquiry and experimentation would qualify and validate what had already been revealed to Muhammad a century prior.

Again, in the author's view, this knowledge, this highly complex knowledge and scientific insight, was revealed to Muhammad from G-d as a blessing of scientific awakening for the benefit of humanity, but also as a "clear and undeniable proof" that the Quran is not something fabricated by Muhammad or anyone else, but clearly the word from The All- Knowing Creator. Lastly, it is the author's opinion that these "proofs" that were revealed to Muhammad in the Quran were so intended because, science in and of itself, represents enlightenment and enhanced education acquired from disciplined inquiry and systematic research; and what better way to introduce scientific enlightenment to the world of man, than through someone who was unschooled and considered unlearned, like Muhammad.

It is commonly understood by those who are familiar and historians alike, that Muhammad was unlettered and unlearned, that is, he was uneducated in any form of structured tutoring, as many others were in the deserts of Mecca. Be not mistaken however, he was not ignorant as in unsophisticated, nor was he uncouth as in uncivilized, not in anyway; just uneducated and unlearned. G-d however, revealed to him a weighty message that would not only validate and affirm the message of Jesus, by calling the hearts and souls of people back to goodness and righteousness, but also a profound message containing potent verses that would ignite a bright light of scientific awakening for humanity. Let us now take a close look at some of the "clear proofs" that were revealed to Muhammad in the Quran.

AUTHENTICITY OF THE QURAN

The first and perhaps most profound "clear proof" that was revealed to Muhammad in the Quran, pertains to the subject of embryology and human reproduction. There are several verses throughout the Quran which speak to and clearly describe the intriguing development of human reproduction. These verses that were revealed to Muhammad describing the intricate aspects and sequenced processes of human reproduction, were not known at the time of Muhammad. What man thought of the subject at that time was primarily composed of myth, unfounded hypothesis, and superstition. For one to have correctly understood and accurately describe the highly complexed processes involved in human reproduction, he would at least have had to (1) invent or at least possess a microscope, (2) be well versed in such sciences as anatomy, physiology, embryology, and even obstetrics, and (3) have been well-schooled and highly educated to cogently present all the above; Muhammad however, was obviously not accessible to any of these!

Yet we find in the Quran several verses describing the exact components, stages, and meticulous processes of human reproduction that were not proven and confirmed by advanced technology until many years after Muhammad. The very first message of inspiration that came to Muhammad by way of the angel Gabriel included vital information about human reproduction. The first message of inspiration that came to Muhammad through the angel Gabriel, you may recall, happened while Muhammad was seeking solitude and contemplation in the cave Hira. The first message to Muhammad was,

"Read and Recite, in the Name of Your Lord and Cherisher who created, created man from a germ cell that clings and is attached (alaq), Read and Recite, for your Lord is Most Bountiful and Generous, He who has taught by the pen, taught man what he was before not knowing". (Quran, chapter 96 verses 1-5) [1]

In several other verses throughout the Quran, the subject of human reproduction imparts knowledge that was not known at the time. Here are other reference verses for review;

(1) "O mankind, if you are in doubt about the Resurrection, consider that We created you out of dust (turaab), then out of sperm (nuutfatin), then out of a leech-like germ cell clinging (alaq), then out of a morsel of flesh, partly formed and partly unformed (fetus), in order that We may manifest Our power to you". (Quran, chapter 22, verse 5) [2]

(2) "Verily We created man from a quintessence of clay (wet earth), Then We placed him as a drop of sperm in a place of rest firmly fixed; Then We developed the sperm into a leech-like germ cell clinging, then developed the leech-like germ cell into a fetus (partly formed and partly unformed), then We made from that fetus bones, then clothe the bones with flesh, then We developed it into another created being, so Blessed be Allah, The Best to Create and give form". (Quran, chapter 23, verses 12-14)

(3) "It is He who has created you from dust, then from a sperm drop, then from a leech-like germ cell clinging (alaq), then does He deliver you from the womb of your

mother as a child, then He makes it so that you grow to reach the age of full maturation, then He makes it so that you grow old, though there are some of you who die before this point, so that you may complete your appointed term and grow in wisdom". (Quran, chapter 40, verse 67).

(4) "Verily We created man from an *(amshaj)*, a mixed sperm drop of both properties from the male and female, so that We may test him. So We gave him the faculties of hearing and seeing". (Quran, chapter 76, verse 2).[3]

(5) "He makes you in the wombs of your mothers, in stages one after another, in three veils of darkness. Such is Allah, your Lord and Cherisher: to Him belongs all Dominion and Sovereignty. There is none worthy of worship but He, how then are you turned away from your true focus and center. (Quran, chapter 39, verse 6).[4]

The Quran Unveiled Mystery and Enhanced Science

The verses you have just read from the Quran describing and illustrating fetal growth and development were revealed to Muhammad nearly 14 centuries ago. Attention is drawn to key Arabic terms in these verses from the Quran that not only mention exact physical components involved in human reproduction, but also the description of precise and sequential stages in the early conceptual and developmental process. Please note, this exact knowledge was not known at the time, and all that existed among those considered highly educated was mere theory and conjecture without any convincing evidence. The 5th reference verse we just cited from the Quran mentions that we were made in the womb of our mother in stages, one after another, in three veils of darkness. What is the significance of this verse?

The significance of this verse is that it further proves that this information could only have been conveyed to Muhammad from the Creator alone. No one anywhere at that time had an in depth and exact knowledge of the 3 layers of the mothers' womb, called the uterus. The three veils of darkness mentioned in this verse, pertaining to the physical (womb) of our mother, is referring to the 3 trimester periods of pregnancy; but it also pertains to the 3 anatomical layers that protect the developing embryo, (1) the mothers' anterior abdominal wall, (2) the wall of the uterus, and (3) the amniochorionic membrane. It is common knowledge today that the womb (uterus) of the woman is comprised of 3 distinct layers, (1) the endometrium, the myometrium, and the perimetrium. These three distinct layers of the uterus nurture and protect the growing embryo. Again, this is common knowledge today, however at the time that this was made known to Muhammad in the Quran, no one anywhere knew this.

It is well documented that during the Middle Ages and for several centuries after, only myth and unfounded speculation existed concerning the exact processes of human conception and reproduction. In fact, the chronicles of history show that it was not until 1651 when William Harvey, an English scientist and physician greatly influenced by Aristotle, published his book entitled, *"On the Generation of Animals"*, that provided the foundation for modern day embryology.[5] If you were to closely examine the components and intricate processes of human reproduction as described in modern day embryology, and then carefully read the verses we have just cited from the Quran that were revealed to Muhammad, you would have to ask yourself this perplexing question. How was Muhammad, (1) without the possession of a microscope to identify the properties of sperm and ovum, (2) without the aid of any advanced technology such as ultrasound sonography to view images of fetal growth and development, and especially (3) without having any formal education to understand the principles of biology, physiology, or even obstetrics and embryology; how was Muhammad able to know this highly complexed information and intelligently write it in a book over 1400 years ago, when it was not until 1651, well over a thousand years later, when the basis of modern day embryology was being formulated by William Harvey?

The answer to this question is clear and simple, not ambiguous or complexed. The answer is this, no one else but G-d, The All-Knowing Creator, could have imparted this type of knowledge to Muhammad approximately 1400 years ago, at a time when no one else was privy to this highly complexed insight. The author contends once again, that G-d specifically imparted knowledge to Muhammad of certain natural and scientific phenomenon that was not known at the time. The author further asserts that G-d conveyed to him the exact description and sequence of certain occurrences as an undebatable proof that the message of the Quran could only be from one source, G-d, The Creator Supreme, The All Knowing, The All Wise, Lord of all worlds and systems of knowledge.

The Seven Layers of the Sky and Seven Layers of the Earth

There are several verses in the Quran that announced yet another scientific observation that was not common knowledge at the time that it was made known to Muhammad. On at least four separate occasions, select verses were revealed to Muhammad conveying knowledge of our heavens (skies) and of the earth that was not known at the time. In the Quran, we read,

(1) "Blessed be He in Whose Hand is Dominion, and He over all things has Power; He who created death and life, that He may try which of you is best in deed, and He is The Exalted in Might, The Oft-Forgiving; He who created the seven heavens one above another: no want of order or proportion will you see in the creation of The Most Gracious, so turn your vision again, do you see any flaw?, again turn your vision a second time: your vision will come back to you dull and discomfiting, in a state worn out". (chapter 67 verses 1-4)

(2) "Do you not see that Allah has created the seven heavens one above another". (chapter 71 verse 15)

(3) "It is He (Allah) who created for you all things that are on earth; then He turned to the heaven and made them into seven firmaments, and of all things He (Allah) has perfect knowledge. (chapter 2 verse 29)

(4) "Allah is He who created the seven firmaments and of the earth a similar number. Through the midst of them all descends His command: that you may know that Allah has power over all things, and that Allah comprehends all things in His Knowledge". (chapter 65 verse 12)

It is common knowledge today that the sky above us is comprised of seven layers, one above another.[1] Not surprisingly, each of these seven layers are not only identified and distinguished by their distance from the earth, but more particularly, they are distinguished by such properties such as their differential pressures, gaseous composition, their absorption of high frequency radio waves, etc. The seven layers are known in physical geography as (1) Trophosphere, (2) Tropopause, (3) Stratosphere, (4) Stratopause, (5) Mesosphere, (6) Mesopause, and (7) Thermosphere. It is also common knowledge today that our earth is comprised of seven layers. The earth's seven layers are (1) crust, (2) lithosphere, (3) upper mantle, (4) asthenosphere, (5) lower mantle, (6) outer core, and (7) inner core.[2]

These scientific observations and the validated proofs of the seven layers of the skies and seven layers of the earth are readily accessible to everyone in contemporary physical geography, earth science, astronomy, geology, and the like. These branches of study and the vast amount of scientific knowledge however, were not available 1400 years ago when the Quran was conveyed to Muhammad. Therefore, the author asks each reader to carefully ponder this question. How could Muhammad, who was unlearned and uneducated, have known 1400 years ago that there are seven layers to the skies above, and that there are seven layers of the earth below, when such information was not "discovered" until 20th century technology was available to confirm such? The only One who could have imparted this type of knowledge to Muhammad of the heavens and the earth, is The One who created the heavens and the earth; The Creator Supreme!

How Did Muhammad Know The Universe Was Expanding?

*U*ndoubtedly, the fields of astronomy and astrophysics have provided a plethora of information about our awe-inspiring universe. By way of travel in space, tireless research, and profound observations substantiated by physics and astronomy; there are numerous fascinating discoveries that have been introduced and expounded on in the field of science, particularly astronomy.

Interestingly, there is yet another highly unique scientific observation that had already been revealed to Muhammad in the Quran 1400 years ago, long before it was ever theorized and later proven. This highly unique scientific observation and discovery we are referring to is about the expansion of our universe!

Early astronomers and physicists alike conceived of our universe as being "static", and that it was not expanding or contracting.[1] They perceived the universe as being composed primarily of the visible stars, known planets at the time, our sun, the moon, and they believed that all of this was motionless. This was the commonly held view during the 19th and 20th century.[1] As fate would have it, and as curiosity, research, and technology evolved, this idea of a "static" universe soon became obsolete. Upon further inquiry by brilliant minds like Albert Einstein in 1917, Georges LeMaitre in 1927, and finally Edwin Hubble in 1929, it was proven that our universe is not static at all, but on the contrary, it is and has been steadily expanding.[2]

The author therefore asks each reader to ponder yet another thought-provoking question. How could Muhammad, who was unlearned and uneducated, without the possession of a highly advanced telescope and without even the slightest clue of astronomy or astrophysics, have known 1400 years ago that the universe was steadily expanding, when this unique fact was not discovered and proven until 1929 by Edwin Hubble with the aid of the Hooker telescope?[3] In chapter 51 verse 47 of the Quran, we read the following verse that was revealed to Muhammad;

"And it is We who have constructed the heaven with might, and verily, it is We who are steadily expanding it".[4]

As you can see, it had already been stated in the Quran 1400 years ago that the universe was steadily expanding, and yet, though Georges LeMaitre proposed this same idea in 1927, and although Albert Einstein initially refused to change from his "static" idea of the universe, but later finally agreed that it is steadily expanding; it was not until 1929 when Edwin Hubble proved it with the help of the Hooker telescope. His discovery and computations subsequently revolutionized the field of astronomy and astrophysics. His brilliant discovery however, had already been revealed in the Quran to an unlearned and uneducated man by the name of Muhammad, hundreds of years prior!

The Barrier between Fresh Water and Salt Water

*A*nother scientific phenomenon that was not known at the time, but was revealed to Muhammad in the Quran, relates to the subject of Oceanography. If you were to explore the study of Oceanography, you would eventually embark upon the subject that discusses the barrier, also referred to as partition, that separates and/or divides fresh water from salt water. For hundreds of years, man had been perplexed and unable to explain how or why this occurs.

Contemporary Oceanography confirms that as it relates to the meeting of fresh water with salt water, there is a barrier/partition that is actively present, although the human eye can barely see this unique feature. Modern science has discovered that in places where two different seas meet, there is a barrier between them. This barrier divides the two seas so that each sea has its own temperature, salinity, and density. In addition, modern science has discovered that in estuaries, where fresh (sweet) and salt water meet, the situation is somewhat different from what is found in places where two seas meet. It has been discovered that what distinguishes fresh water from salt water in estuaries is a "pycnocline zone with a marked density discontinuity separating the two layers."[1] This partition (zone of separation) has a different salinity from fresh water and from salt water.[1]

There are at least 3 references in the Quran that were revealed to Muhammad over 1400 years ago, which had already conveyed this scientific information. In the Quran we read,

"He has set free the two bodies of flowing water, meeting together; between them is a "barrier" which they do not transgress". (chapter 55, verses 19-20)

"It is He Who has let free the two bodies of flowing water, one sweet and palatable, and the other salty and bitter: yet has He made a barrier between them; a partition that is forbidden to be passed". (chapter 25, verse 53)

"Or, who has made the earth firm to live in, made rivers in its midst, set thereon mountains immovable, and made a "separating bar" between the two bodies of flowing water? Can there be another g-d besides Allah? Nay, most of them know not". (chapter 27, verse 61)

We see from the 3 distinct verses of the Quran that were revealed to Muhammad, this phenomenon of a barrier / partition separating fresh and salt water is clearly stated. It was also established earlier in this book that Muhammad was unlearned or tutored in any form of structured education, before the advent of the Quran. We also know today that much of the discoveries upon which contemporary Oceanography is derived, was not known before the Challenger expedition of 1872 -76. Per Wikipedia, "As recently as the late 19th century, human knowledge of the oceans was confined to the topmost few fathoms of the water and a small amount of the bottom, mainly in shallow areas. Sailors and scientists knew almost nothing of the ocean depths".

The obvious question therefore is, how could Muhammad have known 1400 years ago that there is a barrier / partition that separates salt water from fresh water in our seas and oceans, when such highly complexed "under water research" was not conducted until the Challenger expedition of 1872? How is it humanly possible that Muhammad, who was not an oceanographer in the least, nor a marine biologist, nor a surveyor in any manner, how could he possibly have known such refined information pertaining to Oceanography, when such information was not available until hundreds of years later? The only intelligent and plausible explanation is that this information was conveyed to Muhammad by The One who made the seas and oceans; The Grand Architect, The All-Knowing Creator.

The author contends therefore, that this information regarding the barrier / partition that pertains to salt water and fresh water is another proof of the authenticity of the Quran's origin and validity. This, like the other scientific examples cited, was conveyed to Muhammad to enlighten man in diverse fields of scientific inquiry, but also to validate for those who have doubts, that the message of the Quran could only have been from G-d, The All Knowing, Creator Supreme.

The Defeat and Victory of the Roman Empire

As mentioned at the beginning of this book, the author has always been fascinated and intrigued by world history. As early as the 6th grade, this intrigue and fascination was not merely with just the curiosity and interest of significant historical events and the persons involved. More specifically, it was a fascination and intrigue about the correlation of historical events, the unique similarities in the key persons involved, and lastly, with the probability and sometimes predictability of future events based upon observable patterns.

Speaking of the predictability of future events, the author was further convinced of the creditability and authenticity of the Quran, upon learning that the victory of the Roman Empire over the Persian Empire had already been "predicted" and fore told in the Quran at least nine years before it had come to pass.[1]

Chronicles of history detail the ongoing conflicts and battles fought between the Byzantine Empire and the Persian Empire, which span over many years. The culmination of one such battle ended as a major defeat for the Roman Empire, so much so, the Persians subsequently conquered Mesopotamia, the Caucus, Syria, Anatolia, Chalcedon, Palestine, Egypt, parts of Asia Minor, and even Ancyra, a significant military installation in central Anatolia. As you would imagine, this was a significant defeat and indicated a major collapse of the Roman Empire.

Yet, despite such loss, it was during this same time that a prophetic message was conveyed to Muhammad in the Quran announcing the defeat of the Roman Empire, but also predicting that in about 3 to 9 years they would once again be victorious! Not surprisingly, when the news of the Roman defeat spread through Arabia, it was joyously celebrated by the predominant people of Mecca, but it was disheartening news to Muhammad and his followers. It was disheartening to Muhammad and his followers because, although not identical in every belief, Christianity, which was the religion of the Roman Empire, was more representative of monotheism than the Zoroastrianism of the Persians. The overwhelming people of Mecca, you may recall, were still heavily consumed with paganism and idolatry; and therefore, felt a sense of "commonality" with Persian Zoroastrianism, which was more akin to dualism than monotheism.

At the defeat of the Roman Empire, the following verses were revealed to Muhammad in the Quran:

"The Roman Empire has been defeated in a land close by, but they, even after this defeat of theirs, will soon be victorious in 3 to 9 years. With Allah is the Decision, in the past and in the future; on that day, shall the Believers rejoice". (Quran chapter 30, verses 2-4)

As you might imagine, this message in the Quran predicting that the Roman Empire would soon be victorious in 3 to 9 years, was perceived by the people of Mecca as a "litmus test" of the Qurans' validity and authenticity. If the prediction proved false, the popular majority of Mecca would have considered it convincing proof that the Quran was mere heresy from Muhammad's imagination, and therefore lacking merit. If, on the other hand this prediction proved true, then they would be compelled by higher reasoning to reconsider their views and acknowledge the merit and authenticity of the Quran. In so doing, they would realize that this prediction in the Quran was not mere conjecture or "unfounded prophecy" from Muhammad, but that it was an irrefutable prediction from The One who knows the beginning and finality of all future events, The One G-d!

As the chronicles of history show, in approximately 7 to 9 years from the time these verses were revealed to Muhammad in the Quran, the Roman Empire did in fact become victorious. With persistence and strategy, after rebuilding and strengthening his army, Heraclius led the Romans to a successful victory over the Persians in a decisive battle called the Battle of Nineveh in 627.[2]

The author asks each reader therefore to ponder the following question. How could Muhammad, after learning that the Roman Empire had been defeated, have known for absolute certain that in 3 to 9 years they would be victorious? Even more, how could Muhammad have known that this would occur within the specific time span mentioned in the Quran, of 3 to 9 years? History speaks for itself, the proof is in the pudding. The only logical explanation plausible is that this prediction in the Quran was not from Muhammad himself, it could only be from The One who conveyed the Quran to Muhammad, The One who knows the beginning and finality of all future events, The One G-d.

There are several other additional references in the Quran that the author considers to be "irrefutable evidence" and "convincing proofs", that it (The Quran) could only be from one source, The One G-d, The All-Knowing Creator. For the sake of brevity however, the author has decided to list these few examples as convincing proof that the message of the Quran revealed to Muhammad, could only be from G-d, The Creator Supreme, who created everything in existence and gave everything its characteristics and intricate properties.

From the 5 examples we have already explored, (1) the intricate description of the early stages of human reproduction, (2) the repeated mentioning of the 7 layers of the atmosphere and the 7 layers of the earth, (3) The mentioning of the "expansion" of the universe, (4) the barrier / partition between salt water and fresh water, and (5) predicting the victory of the Roman Empire within 3 to 9 years after their defeat, all of which was conveyed to Muhammad in the Quran and all of which has been proven to be scientifically and historically factual; it must therefore be intelligently deduced and rationally explained, that this type of information could only have been conveyed to Muhammad from one source, The Creator of the heavens and the earth.

JESUS AND MUHAMMAD PRACTICED FASTING

*R*eturning to our discussion of noted similarities in Jesus and Muhammad, this book would be remiss if we did not include one of the most well-known commonalities observed in the lives of both Jesus and Muhammad, the practice of fasting.

The religious tradition of fasting has always aimed at strengthening the spiritual and moral force within the individual. It was and still is considered a spiritual and mental exercise of sincere faith and persistent will power. The object of fasting is an attempt for one to strengthen their ability to avoid temptation and sin, while seeking to draw nearer to G-d in mind and spirit. Most Christians are familiar with the Biblical account in the New Testament of Jesus fasting 40 days and 40 nights in what was called "the wilderness" (Matthew 4:1-2). In the subsequent verses that follow, it states that Jesus was being tempted by the devil, but at each suggestion and invitation from the devil, Jesus immediately affirmed with strong unwavering conviction, his acknowledgement of and devout commitment to the worship of G-d.

Not surprisingly, Muhammad also fasted. For example, you may recall earlier as we described Muhammad seeking contemplation and solitude away from the abhorrent and pagan customs in Mecca, he would go to a cave called Hira. Muhammad fasted as an approach to finding some degree of moral resolve and spiritual replenishment from the evil and uncouth life of Mecca.

145

It comes as no surprise then, that the subject of fasting was revealed to Muhammad in the Quran in a similar context as was described in the New Testament concerning Jesus in "the wilderness". The following verse found in the Quran reads as such:

> "O you who believe, fasting is prescribed for you, as it was prescribed for those who were before you, that you may guard against evil and learn self-restraint". (Quran chapter 2, verse 183)[1]

A close look at the language of this verse that was revealed to Muhammad, captures the essence and spiritual purpose for which Jesus is reported to have fasted in the Bible. The Biblical account of Jesus fasting 40 days and 40 nights (Matthew 4: 1-2) describes Jesus being led by the Spirit into "the wilderness" to be tempted by the devil. In preparation for this, it says that he fasted 40 days and 40 nights. Sounds like Jesus was fasting this way in hopes of strengthening his spiritual and moral energies even more, for what was to come in terms of temptations and suggestions from the devil.

The author considers it safe to say, "the wilderness" referenced in the narration when Jesus fasted is at least compatible if not comparable, to the wilderness of our present times, with its myriad of vices and all forms of open and subliminal temptations.

It is also at least compatible to the "Jahiliyyah" (Time of Ignorance) during which Muhammad lived in Mecca. For this purpose and for other noble reasons, Muhammad also fasted.

The message therefore that was revealed to Muhammad in the Quran stating that "fasting is prescribed for you, as it was prescribed for those before you, that you may guard against evil and learn self-restraint", makes sense if you think about it. Fasting served as a spiritual and moral vitamin for Jesus and his opposition and fasting also served as a spiritual and moral vitamin for Muhammad and his opposition. It was the same prescription, and just Who do you think is the Prescriber? Who do you think is The One that designed fasting to have such awesome effect and potent benefits? It is The Lord your G-d who is One G-d, who knows all our strengths and all our vulnerabilities.

We identified similar themes and expressions in the prayers of Jesus and Muhammad very early in this book. We then reflected on what is mentioned in what is commonly called "The Lord's Prayer" that Jesus taught, "lead us not into temptation, but deliver us from evil". We then compared that to what is mentioned in the prayer that Muhammad taught, called "The Al Fatiha", "Guide us on the Straight Way, the way of those on whom You have bestowed Your Grace, not the way of those who incur Your wrath, nor the way of those who go astray".

An unbiased look and intelligent comparison of these two expressions in the prayers of Jesus and Muhammad clearly indicate that they are both seeking the same type of help and direction from G-d, and essentially asking for the same thing. It therefore makes perfect sense why both Jesus and Muhammad also had the commonality of fasting; (1) to further strengthen their spiritual and moral propensities, (2) to heighten their awareness and sensitivities of the poor and less fortunate in society, and (3) to better situate their heart, mind, and soul to be guided by G-d away from the vices and subtleties that distract, tempt, and lead one astray.

JESUS AND MUHAMMAD TAUGHT PRINCIPLES OF INTERFAITH

In the often-used opening words of Jesus per the New Testament, the author begins this chapter with the following statement, "He that has ears to hear, let him hear". The topic we are about to discuss concerning both Jesus and Muhammad teaching principles of interfaith, is one that will hopefully (1) help to break down barriers of communication and perception amongst varied faith groups, (2) identify the "greater good" to be achieved from bipartisan recognition and unintimidated participation, and (3) illustrate from scripture once again, that Jesus and Muhammad are as 2 Rays of The Same Light!

During the author's research of the New Testament and the Quran, key verses in both scriptures were observed that presented similar aspects, illustrated like principles, and complemented each other on the concept of interfaith. While this subject of "interfaith" maybe obscure, new, or foreign to some; it is well understood, respected, and highly endorsed by many more who are both comprehensive and versatile in their religious thinking and understanding. Being versatile and comprehensive in our religious thinking is a must, living in a world as diverse as ours. It is for this reason the author offers the following reference verse from the New Testament spoken by Jesus;

And his mother and his brothers came, and standing outside they sent to him and called him; and a crowd was sitting around him, and they said to him, "your mother and your brothers are outside seeking you", and he answered them, "who are my mother and my brothers?" And looking about at those who sat around him he said, "Here are my mother and my brothers! For whoever does the will of G-d, he is my brother and sister and mother". (New Testament, Mark 3: 31-35)

Based upon the context and setting of the above-mentioned verse, the author considers it safe to say that from the literal reading, Jesus obviously meant no sacrilege, discourtesy, or disrespect what so ever toward his beloved biological mother Mary or his biological brothers, (whose names are not mentioned).[1] The fact of the matter is that in these reported words, it is apparent that Jesus was trying to drive home a much more significant idea and emphasize a point of much larger magnitude.

By reasoning and inference, these words from Jesus should provoke considerable thought and draw our attention to a much broader idea of our significant relations with people. In this setting, Jesus has placed the same esteem and cherished value that we would naturally have for our biological mother, sister, and brother, with "who so ever shall do the will of G-d".

When we think of our mother, sister, or brother, we naturally consider and value the close ties of relationship along blood lines of marriage, family, children, etc. However, the words in this verse compel everyone who identifies with and asserts to follow Jesus, to broaden their outlook in the larger society of man. Remember, per the words stated by Jesus, the prerequisite for this broadened outlook is, "who so ever shall do the will of G-d". From this perspective, your brothers and sisters will naturally consist of those doing the will of G-d from among your immediate religious affiliates that you do know, and based on this verse, your brothers and sisters will consist equally from among many others who are also doing the will of G-d, who are not of your immediate religious affiliation, that you may not know. Again, the prerequisite is "who so ever shall do the will of G-d, such is your brother and sister".[2]

Not surprisingly Muhammad also advocated this humanitarian idea, taught noteworthy principles of interfaith, and provided relevant examples of such. In addition to advocating the fair and equitable treatment of women and teaching about equality among the races and ethnicities of society, Muhammad also taught on the principle of interfaith. As we explore the principle that Jesus expressed in the New Testament regarding "who so ever shall do the will of G-d, such is my brother and my sister", please note that to Muhammad were revealed several verses in the Quran that were to "reiterate and further expound" on this same principle Jesus advocated, and even more; gave direct references to various people of faith. Please reflect upon the following verses from the Quran that were revealed to Muhammad:

"Those who believe in the Quran, and those who follow the Jewish scripture, and the Christians and the Sabians, any who believe in Allah (G-d) and the Last Day, and work righteousness, shall have their reward with their Lord; on them shall be no fear, nor shall they grieve".[3] (Quran 2:62)

"O mankind, We created you from a single pair of a male and female, and made you into nations and tribes, that you may know each other, not that you may despise each other; verily the most honored of you in the sight of Allah is the most righteous of you; and Allah has full knowledge and is well acquainted with all things". (Quran 49:13)

"To each of you is a goal to which Allah turns him, then strive as in a race towards all that is good, where so ever you are, Allah will bring you together, for Allah has power over all things". (Quran 2:148)

"Nay, whoever submits his whole self to Allah and is a doer of good, he will get his reward with his Lord, on such shall be no fear, nor shall they grieve" (Quran 2:112)

A careful review of the above-mentioned verses from the Quran that Muhammad taught, show consistency and congruence with the principle that Jesus taught. Jesus taught that who so ever shall do the will of G-d is to be considered your brother and your sister, providing they are in fact doing the will of G-d, and of course, providing you yourself are doing the will of G-d!

These concise but potent verses that were revealed to Muhammad in the Quran clearly "reiterate" the same principle that Jesus spoke of, as well as provide the social context through which to envision its demonstration. The verses from Jesus in Mark 3:31-35 of the New Testament brilliantly announce the foundational concept and principle of interfaith. The verses from the Quran that Muhammad taught serve as the complimentary synthesis, and provides the blue print, by directly addressing the merit of sincere believers from varied faith groups, all of whom are doing the will of G-d.

The author recommends a detailed review of these concise but potent verses that were revealed to Muhammad in the Quran, that show likeness and congruence to what Jesus taught in Mark 3:31-35.

"Those who believe in the Quran, and those who follow the Jewish scripture, and the Christians and the Sabians, any who believe in Allah and the Last Day, and work righteousness, shall have their reward with their Lord; on them shall be no fear, nor shall they grieve".[1] (Quran 2:62)

"O mankind, We created you from a single pair of a male and female, and made you into nations and tribes, that you may know each other, not that you may despise each other; verily the most honored of you in the sight of Allah is the most righteous of you; and Allah has full knowledge and is well acquainted with all things". (Quran 49:13)

"To each of you is a goal to which Allah turns him, then strive as in a race towards all that is good, where so ever you are, Allah will bring you together, for Allah has power over all things". (Quran 2:148)

"Nay, whoever submits his whole self to Allah and is a doer of good, he will get his reward with his Lord, on such shall be no fear, nor shall they grieve" (Quran 2:112)

The author contends that if you carefully read and understand the verses of what Jesus said, regarding "whoever shall do the will of G-d, such is my brother and my sister", and then carefully read these concise but potent verses from the Quran that Muhammad taught; you would have to admit that they "shake hands" with each other and clearly show agreement and consistency. The author contends that these verses that were revealed to Muhammad in the Quran, addressing the merit of devout members from different faith groups all doing the will of G-d, should inspire hope and optimism for improved relations amongst members of varied faith groups.

The four verses we have cited from the Quran that Muhammad taught obviously merit further elucidation. Our discussion on Jesus and Muhammad regarding "interfaith" was not intended to simply "touch upon the surface". The author considers this subject to be so vitally important, socially relevant, and to be of such high priority; that it warrants unbiased and comprehensive discussion. With an open and impartial mind, as we closely inspect each verse from the Quran that Muhammad taught, its relevance and connection to the message of Jesus becomes clearer and ultra-apparent.

1. "Those who believe in the Quran, and those who follow the Jewish scripture, and the Christians and the Sabians, any who believe in Allah and the Last Day, and work righteousness, shall have their reward with their Lord; on them shall be no fear, nor shall they grieve". (Quran 2:62)

This verse from the Quran that Muhammad taught is consistent with the message of Jesus when he said, "who so ever shall do the will of G-d, such is my brother and my sister." It recognizes and establishes the "legitimacy" of those who believe in the Quran (Muslims), those who follow the Jewish scripture (Jews), those who are Christians, and even others such as the Sabians, and it culminates by stipulating that so long as they truly believe in G-d and the Last Day (Judgement), and they live a life that "WORKS RIGHTEOUSNESS"; that they all shall have their reward with their Lord, on them shall be no fear, nor shall they grieve.

The message here is that G-d is "The Judge", and He is equally accessible by Muslims, Christians, Jews, and even others like the Sabians. He wants us all to be able to exercise our individual religious autonomy, but kindly recognize and honor the "legitimacy" of your other brothers and sisters from other faith groups. He wants us to do this by remembering that He alone is THE JUDGE, and we are all subjects in HIS COURT ROOM! If a person calls their self a Christian, and he or she truly believes in G-d and the Last Day and conduct their self in righteousness, they will get their full reward from their Lord.

If a man or woman follows the Jewish scripture and calls their self a Jew, and that person truly believes in G-d and the Last Day and conduct their self in righteousness, they will get their full reward from their Lord. If a person follows the Quran and calls their self a Muslim, and that person truly believes in G-d and the Last Day, and conduct their self in righteousness, that person will get their full reward from their Lord. The "key" is regardless of what you call yourself, if you truly believe in G-d, The Creator of the heavens and the earth, and believe in the Last Day, which is the time that only G-d knows when all that presently exists must end and we all must give an account of our deeds; and then you WALK what you TALK, that is, if you live a life "seeking" to be righteous as would please G-d; then it should not be hard for you to respect that same spirit and legitimacy in someone else from a different faith group, who also believes in G-d and likewise tries to live a life of righteousness such as pleases G-d. In the context of Jesus words from the New Testament and the reference verse from the Quran, such is your brother and your sister in the bigger picture! This bigger picture is the same bigger picture Jesus was trying to convey in our Biblical reference verse when he said, "who so ever shall do the will of G-d, such is my brother and my sister".

Another point worth mentioning here is that for each of the faith groups mentioned in this verse from the Quran, it says that each of them that truly believe in G-d and the Last Day, and work righteousness, will get their reward from their Lord. The author would like to emphasize the part that says, "from their Lord".

In earlier chapters of this book, we explored the similarity and likeness of Jesus and Muhammad both teaching that "The Lord your G-d is one G-d". That means that the same Lord who will reward the sincere Jew is the same Lord who will reward the sincere Christian. As well, the same Lord who will reward the sincere Christian is the same Lord who will reward the sincere Muslim, because there is but One Lord who we ALL are accountable to. Remember, it is on record that both Jesus and Muhammad taught "The Lord your G-d is but One G-d". Therefore, so long as each of them truly believe in G-d and the Last Day, and they live a life seeking to do the will of G-d by working righteousness, each of them will get their reward, on them will be no fear, nor shall they grieve. No one individual or faith group has the upper hand over the other, except in righteousness such that pleases G-d and that does His Will. Let us proceed to explore the second reference verse:

2. "O mankind, We created you from a single pair of a male and female, and made you into nations and tribes, that you may know each other, not that you may despise each other; verily the most honored of you in the sight of Allah is the most righteous of you; and Allah has full knowledge and is well acquainted with all things". (Quran 49:13)

This verse from the Quran that Muhammad taught is also consistent with the principle that Jesus taught. In Mark 3:31-35 of the New Testament, Jesus taught that "who so ever shall do the will of G-d, such is my brother and my sister". This verse from the Quran captures that same humanitarian posture, but also goes further by reminding everyone that we all came from a single pair of a male and a female (Adam and Eve), and then by the subsequent plan of G-d over time and circumstances, we were made into nations and tribes (different cultures and ethnicities) so that we would get to know each other, not despise each other. This expression in the Quran "to get to know each other and not despise each" in Arabic is "lita aarafu".[4]

So, for the wide awake and attentive reader, G-d is inferring here that He purposely and willfully intended that there be cultural, religious, and ethnic diversity! In His Majestic Plan and Perfect Wisdom, He is telling us here in this verse that He did not want or intend everyone to be of the same nationality or ethnicity, having the same skin pigment and features, having the same identical culture, speaking the same language, having the same culinary appetites and favorite dishes, having the same names and such; no, not at all. He wanted us to have enough of these select differences of social diversity, but He wanted us to have enough "Common Sense and Spiritual Sense", to recognize that "The Best" of anyone of us, is not the White man or the Black man, not the Arab or the non-Arab, or any other exclusive race or ethnic group that inhabits this spacious earth.

Nor is "The Best" of anyone among us the one who necessarily calls them self a Muslim, Christian, Jew, or any other exclusive religious identity. "The Best" in the sight of G-d, is the one who is most obedient to G-d, most conscious of pleasing G-d in their conduct, and most consistent at doing the Will of G-d in their everyday life. In other words, the proof is in the content, not the label. This verse from the Quran therefore, not only reiterates the principle of interfaith that both Jesus and Muhammad advocated, but it also reinforces a portion of the message given by Muhammad on Mount Arafat in his Last Sermon about equality among the races. Let us now proceed to our third reference verse:

3. "To each of you is a goal to which Allah turns him, then strive as in a race towards all that is good, where so ever you are, Allah will bring you together, for Allah has power over all things". (Quran 2:148)

This verse from the Quran that Muhammad taught is also consistent with the message of Jesus found in Mark 3:31-35. Jesus taught that "who so ever shall do the will of G-d, such is my brother and my sister". In congruence with that idea, G-d conveyed to Muhammad this verse also to reinforce what Jesus taught. Basically, it is saying that to each of you (Muslims, Christians, Jews, and other believers) there is a goal to which G-d directs you.

Whatever goal and objective one person or group maybe working towards, if it is good, beneficial for the betterment of the community and society, and pleasing to G-d; then it will directly or indirectly contribute in some way to the "good" that other people are also doing. As a principle, good anywhere, provides wholesome support and helps to inspire good everywhere. So therefore, work and strive as in a race and constructive competition, towards ALL THAT IS GOOD. If our works are indeed "good" in the sight of G-d, then it is doing the will of G-d and as the verse says, "where so ever you are, G-d will bring you together".

This doesn't mean that G-d wants to convert everyone to Christianity, Judaism, or Islam, no, not at all. That is not necessary or even the objective. G-d is saying here that if you are all sincere and strive as in a race towards all that is GOOD where ever you are, then because of the sincerity and excellence of that GOODNESS, He will bring us together in MIND and SPIRIT. This sense of being together in mind and spirit with someone from another walk of faith who is also striving towards all that is good for the service to G-d, is part of that bigger picture that Jesus spoke of in the New Testament, and what is also apparent here in this verse from the Quran.

The verse ended by saying "where so ever you are, G-d will bring you together". This statement warrants brief discussion.

In our society, many people of faith have adopted the attitude that unless you "convert" to their faith group or denomination, you are (1) not as favored by G-d as they are, (2) not legitimately recognized and acceptable to G-d, and/or (3) that you are even doomed to punishment and damnation. Not surprisingly, the people who subscribe to any of these views, whether consciously or subconsciously, are often the very ones who consider themselves to be "model followers" of Jesus and Muhammad! As you may recall however, anyone possessing any of these attitudes is clearly in opposition and not conforming to the true spirit of what Jesus said regarding "who so ever shall do the Will of G-d, such is my brother and my sister". As well, they are equally not in agreement with the message and spirit of the Quran. This is exactly why our verse cited from the Quran is vitally important as a reference, for in this verse, G-d says, "where so ever you are, G-d will bring you together".

The average reader may ponder on this and ask, "ok, if this is true, how is G-d going to bring us together if we are in different religions and different denominations, how is that even possible"? To understand the answer to this question, simply call to mind the teachings of Jesus in the New Testament when he said, "who so ever does the will of G-d, such is my brother and my sister"; and also call to mind the teachings of Muhammad in the Quran that says, "To each of you is a goal to which G-d turns him, then strive as in a race towards all that is good, where so ever you are, G-d will bring you together, for G-d has power over all things".

The author prompts each reader to carefully consider the teachings of Jesus where he said, "who so ever shall do the will of G-d, such is my brother and my sister. Now with that principle as a foundation, envision a scenario for example, where a group of concerned Christians, Muslims, Jews, and even other religious affiliates, came together at a community center for the express purpose of identifying ways to feed and provide food and services to the homeless in our impoverished communities. Imagine each of them respectfully engaging and intelligently communicating with each other as a united joint task force, working together on the same agenda, to feed and provide services to the homeless. No one is concerned or occupied with trying to debate each other, no one competing with the other trying to "convert" the other, no one seeking discord or means for difference; rather, each one is simply seeking to do the will of G-d and care for the homeless.

Now take that same model and envision a similar coming together of sincere and concerned Christians, Muslims, Jews, and others in another city, who have come together for the express purpose of establishing viable youth centers that provide wholesome activities for our early youth and young adults. As they eagerly brainstorm and draw from the collective input of ideas for programs and activities to be implemented, they identify a healthy balance of sport and recreational activities, together with educational modules that raises the youth awareness of personal goal setting, cultural diversity, community involvement, preparatory job skills, etc. Once again, they have all come together for the select purpose of providing wholesome activities and programs for the youth and young adults in the neighborhood and broader community.

No one is seeking discord or topics of discussion to divide each other about belief differences, no one is blaming the other or fault-finding the other, no one faith group is boasting of being better or more favored than the other faith group, no one is debating about who is right or who is wrong. In this setting they all are right, and the reason is because they are doing the Will of G-d by serving the needs of the community, which indirectly contributes to the excellent human capital in the broader society. For each of them, it was their genuine concern to make a difference and a better change in the world around them, that brought them together with brothers and sisters from other faith groups. It's like they all became "The Good Samaritan".

In Luke 10: 25-37 of the New Testament, Jesus offers the parable of "The Good Samaritan" to answer the question asked of him, "who is my neighbor"? This well-known biblical parable describes a man who was traveling from Jerusalem to Jericho. During his 17-mile journey he was robbed, stripped, and severely beaten; so much so, he was left half dead. Subsequently as he was lying half dead on the road, a priest happened to be traveling the same route, however when he saw the man lying there on the road, he passed by on the other side of the road.

Soon thereafter a Levite happened to be traveling the same route also, but he too after seeing the man lying there, simply passed by on the other side of the road. Then a Samaritan happened to be traveling down the same road, but when he saw the man lying there half dead, he was immediately moved with genuine care and utmost compassion. His genuine care prompted his attention to first attend to what was obvious, the man's physical state of bodily bruises. He therefore offered immediate first aid in the form of dressing his wounds and treating them with oil and wine. Then, prompted even further by the spirit of compassion, he put the man on his own

163

animal to transport him to a nearby inn to take further care of him. The next day he paid two denarii to the inn keeper and said, "take care of him, and whatever more you spend, I will repay you when I return."

This parable taught by Jesus was his reply when asked, "who is my neighbor?", after teaching that "you shall love the Lord Thy G-d with all your heart, all your soul, all your strength, and with all your mind, and your neighbor as yourself." The moral of this parable obviously, is that if you truly love The Lord Thy G-d with all your heart, soul, strength, and mind; then it is your "inherent nature" and "natural responsibility" to care and show concern to the obvious needs in your community and environment. This is the same moral logic demonstrated in the scenario presented about the Christians, Muslims, Jews, and other religious affiliates who came together as a joint task-force, to show genuine care and utmost compassion for the homeless and youth they identified in their neighborhoods and broader community. In summation, as an interfaith entity, they all fit the description of what Jesus taught in his teaching, "whoever shall do the will of G-d, such is my brother and sister." (Mark 3:35) They equally fit the description of what Muhammad taught in his teaching, "To each of you is a goal to which Allah turns him, then strive as in a race towards all that is good, where so ever you are, Allah will bring

you together, for Allah has power over all things".
(Quran 2:148)

Consider the last reference verse from the
Quran:

4.   "Nay, whoever submits his whole self to Allah and is a
     doer of good, he will get his reward with his Lord, on
     such shall be no fear, nor shall they grieve" (Quran
     2:112)

This last reference verse from the Quran that
Muhammad taught is the icing for the cake; for it
goes right to the point and once again shakes hand
with the message of Jesus in Mark 3:35 of the New
Testament. Jesus taught that "who so ever shall
do the Will of G-d, such is my brother and my
sister". G-d conveyed to Muhammad this verse in
the Quran as another reinforcing testament of the
message of Jesus. This is so because, the idea of
"who so ever shall DO the Will of G-d" that Jesus
said, is consistent if not equivalent, to the idea of
"whoever SUBMITS his whole self to G-d and is a
doer of good" that is in the Quran that Muhammad
taught. Think about it, before you can attempt to
DO the Will of G-d, you must first COMMIT TO and
SUBMIT yourself to G-d, in doing so, your sincere
and humble SUBMISSION will naturally cultivate
within you the mind and spirit to DO the Will of G-
d!

Notice that the verse from the Quran starts
with "whoever submits his "whole self" to G-d and
is a doer of good", and that Jesus started by

saying "whoever shall do the Will of G-d"; clearly the message from the Quran that Muhammad taught and the message from the New Testament that Jesus taught, are emerging from the same central idea and addressing the same moral logic. If you have submitted your "whole self" to G-d, which is the same as saying "all of yourself", not part of yourself, and if you are a "doer of good"; then it is the same as saying you are "doing the will of G-d".

The similar tone and likeness found in the teaching of Jesus and Muhammad on this concept of "interfaith" is obvious, so obvious; it can be readily identified by the average high school student. The author contends that if you were to place the statement from Jesus found in Mark 3:35 of the New Testament, side-by-side with any of the reference verses from the Quran we just explored that Muhammad taught, the average high school student could read them and easily "connect the dots". This is so because, the context in which Jesus uttered his teaching, is parallel to and clearly resembles the context in which Muhammad uttered his teaching. Considering that it is Muhammad who came after Jesus, the message of the Quran therefore not only reaffirms and reiterates the teaching of Jesus; but even more, it carefully describes a visual model of interfaith without bias, where Christians, Muslims, Jews, and even other religious affiliates are considered brothers and sisters, one of another, because they each are doing the Will of G-d.

In summation, the author has demonstrated that both Jesus and Muhammad gave teaching that addressed and established the idea of interfaith. The author deliberated much on the fact that the teaching of Jesus found in Mark 3:31-35 of the New Testament, wisely introduced the idea of interfaith by way of a unique scenario, where he was told that he was being requested of by his brothers and his mother Mary. Jesus, knowing quite well who his biological brothers and mother were, responded by saying to those around him, "whoever that does the Will of G-d, such is my brother, my sister, and mother." The author contends once again that Jesus was not inferring any dishonor or lack of acknowledgement of his physical relations with his biological brothers and beloved mother. On the contrary, as was typical of Jesus in other unique settings like this where he taught through parables and metaphors, he was seeking to expand the minds and thinking of those who say they follow him. As you may imagine, everyone who was present at the time he said these words probably wondered, "hey, doesn't he know who his brothers and his mother Mary are?"

By drawing his audience attention to the significance of "whoever that does the Will of G-d is his brother and sister", Jesus clearly established a principle of faith and action that transcends the shallow constraints and commonly held perspectives, where we consider our "spiritual family of brothers and sisters" to be only those of our inner circle who we may know. When read with an open mind, it becomes apparent that Jesus was inviting and, by way of paradox, encouraging his audience to think "outside of the box."

The author also presented and expounded on four select verses revealed to Muhammad in the Quran that (1) endorsed and reiterated the same moral logic introduced by Jesus in Mark 3:31-35 of the New Testament and (2) gave actual description of members from various walks of faith such as Christians, Muslims, Jews, and even others; who are truly brothers and sisters, one of another, because they are each seeking to do the Will of G-d and are motivated purely by the principle of "doing good". In each of the four reference verses from the Quran that were taught by Muhammad, the author identified the similarity of the moral logic introduced by Jesus from the New Testament.

The authors' hope in discussing this vital subject at length, is to cast light upon a matter often viewed with grave indifference or mere whimsical opinion. The hope also is that more people will see that a unique part of the plan of G-d was to allow Christianity, Judaism, Islam, and other walks of faith to simultaneously co-exist and flourish amongst each other, each with their own unique and distinct autonomy, while its numerous adherents became wiser over time by discovering precious commonalities and shared truths amongst themselves. The author contends that as the colloquial expression has it, "G-d works in mysterious ways", that G-d does indeed work in ways that may appear mysterious to man, but as for G-d, mystery does not exist! On the contrary, the author contends that as illustrated repeatedly throughout nature, G-d often uses "mixture" and "diversity" to convey the message of oneness and fellowship.

Upon this premise, therefore, the author also contends that an integral part of the Awesome Plan of G-d, was to "temporarily allow" various forms of mischief, corruption, social injustice, religious-denominational separation, distrust, hate, prejudice, poverty, RACISM, BIGOTRY, and all the other ugly faces of social- moral decadence, to exist and in fact spread to such an intolerable level in society, that not only invites or suggests the idea of "interfaith", but in fact makes it "urgently necessary" to establish heaven here on earth. The author is aware that for some this may be hard to accept, this idea that G-d would purposely "allow" all the above mentioned detrimental and counter-productive elements to exist and spread in our society. The author however would like to remind each reader that G-d is the All-Knowing, All-Wise, Master-Planner,

169

who created darkness and light, and who knows the past, present, and the future of all things.

By way of the teaching of Jesus in Mark 3:31-35, that was reiterated and duly elaborated on by the teaching of Muhammad in the Quran, there is an ample supply of reasoning and wisdom for anyone who approaches the topic of interfaith. The author has modestly identified much of the synergy and resemblance in Jesus and Muhammad's teaching on this subject. Once again, the author humbly contends that the likeness and complement noted in the teaching of Jesus and Muhammad on this subject is not coincidental or just by random serendipity, but instead, it is because Jesus and Muhammad are as 2 Rays of The Same Light!

EPILOGUE

The initial idea for writing this book was conceived many years ago while I was still active duty in the U.S. Navy. During my naval career, I had the rewarding experience of residing in several cities throughout the United States, as well as several countries abroad. My numerous discussions with fellow Navy and Marine Corps personnel, many of whom were from varied walks of faith and from diverse cultural backgrounds, all contributed to the idea of one day composing an unbiased review of the similar themes and shared perspectives in the teachings of Jesus and Muhammad. The idea for writing this book became more convincing while I was being "educated and inspired" by many of the profound lectures of Imam W. Deen Mohammad, simultaneously as I traveled to such countries as Japan, Spain, Portugal, France, and especially Israel, during the years of 1982 to 1997. It has been a long time coming, and now as a retired veteran, I am grateful to G-d for the discernment and opportunity to share some of the keen observations I have come to understand.

The aforementioned numerous discussions with fellow Navy and Marine Corps personnel, were embellished even more by the thought-provoking discourses I had with some of the indigenous people of Japan, Spain, Portugal, France, and especially Israel. In brief, you would be amazed by what you can learn by visiting different churches, synagogues, and mosques in other parts of the world. Of all places, Israel, more specifically, Haifa, Israel, provided perhaps the most robust spiritual exchange which provided great impetus for writing this book.

At length, I have discussed common themes and similar expositions contained in the teachings of Jesus and Muhammad that undoubtedly will provoke thought and fuel much invigorating discussion. I am convinced however, that the timing is right for a book of this magnitude and subject matter. I have read several periodicals and books comparing Jesus and Muhammad by various authors, but only a few in my honest opinion, if any, have presented a worthy script that truly recognizes and honors the synergy and mutual relevance contained in their teaching.

Considering that I am an avid "fan" of both Jesus and Muhammad equally, my comparative analysis of their teaching was obviously conducted without any favoritism, conflict of interest, or bias for or against either of them. Describing myself as an avid "fan" of both Jesus and Muhammad by the way, comes without any superficial or disingenuous hype about myself or my religious beliefs in any way. Rather, as an "avid fan", and though not "playing" at the same time, I consider both Jesus and Muhammad as "Most Valuable Players" belonging to the same team, and surely not adversaries or opponents as some skeptics would like to portray.

Throughout this book I have drawn from numerous themes, provided side-by-side reference verses from both the New Testament and the Quran, while discussing them in a manner that respects human reasoning and impartiality. Once again, considering that I am an avid "fan" of both Jesus and Muhammad equally, this book was not written with hopes of "converting" or persuading followers of Jesus away from Jesus, at the expense of recognizing the similarities and resemblance of his teaching to Muhammad's. Nor was it written to "hyper-inflate" or exaggerate the significance of Muhammad, at the grand opportunity of showing the significance of his teaching to the teaching of Jesus. It was meticulously composed however, to illustrate the continuity of truth and relativity of diverse subject matter that exists in their shared message.

This book presented numerous themes and highly significant issues addressed by Jesus in the New Testament, that were also addressed and further expounded upon by Muhammad by way of the Quran. Not surprisingly, in many of the references presented in this book, the verbiage uttered by Jesus in the New Testament, was often the same or of compatible verbiage as that expressed by Muhammad in the Quran.

In addition to multiple references throughout this book used to identify similarities and resemblances in the teaching of Jesus and Muhammad, a "gold mine" of shared truths was unveiled as we reviewed the Sermon on the Mount, also called "The Beatitudes" taught by Jesus, and then compared them to the Beatitudes taught by Muhammad, in his Sermon given on Mount Arafat. The likeness of mind, similar attention on moral accountability to G-d and compassionate service in society, together with the obvious synergy identified in their message, both while being delivered from a mountain site; contains too much significance and agreement to be passed off as mere coincidence or random chance.

With humility, I began this book by sharing two distinct qualities I possessed as a young adolescent, (1) I was someone truly fascinated by science, and (2) I was very much interested in and intrigued by world history.

The relevance of this personal observation is that, my fascination was initially with science and all the wonders of natural phenomena, and somehow this eventually gave rise to a keen interest in and intrigue of historical events. However, this was not just a casual interest or surface curiosity. As a sophomore in high school, my interest in science and intrigue with world history became highly zealous and much more intense than that of my peers. For in addition to having a modest interest in world events and the key persons involved, I was highly intrigued by such things as how certain historical events were similar and/or related to other prior events in different places. Grateful to G-d, I seemingly had a natural affinity for identifying contrasts and similarities in historical events and the key persons involved.

Much to my amaze, I often identified paired individuals in history, whose combined contribution present them as what I like to refer to as a "dynamic duo". This view of 2 persons in history serving as a "pair or dynamic duo" was endorsed and further validated during my study of the Quran, in which G-d says that He created everything in pairs! In chapter 51 verse 49 of the Quran, it says, "And of everything, We have created "pairs": that you may receive instruction". My humble position therefore is that, this idea of everything being created in pairs, not only holds true for all created matter, but that it also holds true for the humanities, especially history, as well as for the sciences.

During my undergraduate studies at Clayton State University, my Science and World Studies curriculum provided an exhilarating study of scientific and world events. During this time, I became convinced that many historical events were greatly influenced by the accomplishments of a "duo" or "pair" of two highly significant persons. There are numerous examples of this "dynamic duo" throughout history, a few of these examples can be seen in Louis Pasteur and Antony Van Leeuwenhoek, Johannes Kepler and Isaac Newton, Galileo Galilei and Nicolaus Copernicus, Thomas Edison and Alexander Graham Bell, Albert Einstein and Edwin Hubble, William Harvey and Dr. Charles Drew, Ts' ai lun and Johann Gutenberg, and yes most certainly, in Jesus and Muhammad. Again, my view of 2 similar persons in history serving as a "pair or dynamic duo" was endorsed and validated when I read in the Quran that G-d created everything in pairs.

In each of the above examples, one person is recognized as the one who discovered, identified, and/or initiated something that has become a life changing commodity, resource, and indicator of mans' growth toward enlightenment. The second person in each of the above examples is considered the one who journeyed along the same path of inquiry as the other, confirmed the thinking of the one who came before, obviously found great benefit from the observations and contributions of his predecessor, and subsequently, was favored by G-d with the ability to proceed even further along the path of accomplishment, discovery, and enlightenment.

In this view, that is, the author's view of the "dynamic duo", it is to be understood that the fore runner and the predecessor are of equal status and significance. The one who came along after and proceeded further, is no more significant than the one who came before and initially identified the idea. Although their individual biographies were not identical, one thing is for certain, their combined contributions have left an indelible impact upon the course of human society.

As for the "dynamic duo" of Jesus and Muhammad, this book has attempted to highlight much of the "dynamism" that exits in their shared message. The author has presented numerous examples, as evidenced by the similar messages in the teaching of Jesus and Muhammad, that illustrates their agreement, complement, and likeness of mind and spirit. As emphasized throughout this book, the similarities and resemblance noted in the teaching of Jesus and Muhammad is not by chance or random incident, it is because Jesus and Muhammad are as 2 Rays of The Same Light. **It is noted in one of the reported sayings of Muhammad (the hadith), "Before the end of time, the world will see that Jesus and I are one."**

As an eager student of history and scripture, I am humbly grateful for the opportunity to help illustrate that Jesus and Muhammad are as 2 Rays of The Same Light, and I am among the many who bear witness, **that time has already come!**

Endnotes

Chapter 1

Clearing The Table

1. The English word "God" has an etymology deserving earnest inquiry. Upon review, sources such as Wikipedia.org and Etymology.com indicate the word "God" is derived from (gup, gudis) in Gothic, gud in modern Scandinavian, God in Dutch, and Gott in modern German; which is derived from Proto-Germanic, *gudon*. It is generally agreed upon by informed historians that *gudon* is referring to "The One to whom sacrifices are made" and "That which is invoked." The author contends that, despite the authenticity of the etymology for the word "God", it is not the most preferred term when referring to The Creator; as the reverse spelling of god, is dog.

2. The gesture of giving salutations of "peace be upon him" after mentioning the names of both Jesus and Muhammad, and any of the esteemed prophets and messengers, is a well-known practice in Islam. It is commonly understood that, because Jesus, Muhammad, and all the other distinguished prophets and messengers of G-d were select servants and were bestowed upon such sacred status that only The Creator can give; it is out of high respect and honorable distinction to give such salutations of "peace be upon him" after mentioning their name.

Chapter 2

Why This Title?

1. Our biological and physical existence is dependent upon various intangible resources we too often take for granted. We desperately need light from the sun to dispel the darkness of night and enable us to see during the day. We also need warmth and heat from the sun to remove the discomfort of feeling cold. In a similar manner, our society needs intellectual enlightenment, to see and better understand our prospects for material - technological progress. Equally however, we need the warmth of (moral intelligence and moral sensitivity), so that we can live amongst each other with respect, kindness, and consideration of our fellow-man, as intended by The Creator. Without moral intelligence and moral sensitivity, our material - technological advancements only give the allusion of social progress.

2. Per the New Testament, Jesus is on record for teaching "Love G-d with all your heart, all your soul, all your mind, and your neighbor as yourself". For this love to ever become possible, society must have moral sensitivity as demonstrated in the parable of Jesus about the Good Samaritan.

3. Sincere believers in G-d have a spirit about them that is evident in their mannerism, their speech, and conduct. This spirit is often vivacious and effervescent, and easily identified by other people.

4. Without an active relationship with G-d, man's spiritual component remains void and empty. This

emptiness leaves man prone to seeking to satisfy only physical wants and material needs. An active relationship with G-d infuses man with a spirit that inspires him to yearn for more than only satisfying the physical and biological urges. Though people constantly seek other substitutes, nothing can replace or substitute for an active relationship with G-d, never did, never will.

5. Jesus states that the Kingdom of G-d is within you. As per The Quran, Muhammad taught that G-d will not change your condition until you first change that which is within you (your attitudes, your thinking, your moral and spiritual conscience).

Chapter 3

Jesus and Muhammad: Face-to-face

1. It is commonly presumed by most followers of Jesus, that he taught from what was inherent in his own spiritual and mental faculties. He clearly announces in this verse that the ideas and principles of his teaching ARE NOT from himself, but from THE ONE who sent him.

2. This verse from the Quran informs Muhammad that the Quran was sent down to him and that it confirms the Law of Moses and the Gospel of Jesus, thus showing continuity and relevance to each other. This verse also indicates that Muhammad was also granted "the criterion" (sound

judgement between right and wrong, practical versus impractical, ethical versus unethical, with regards to matters of concern and issues involving individuals and society at large. This description by the way, has inference to what was described of The Comforter, foretold by Jesus in the New Testament.

3. Media coverage of "terrorist attacks" committed by persons who call themselves Muslims are always referred to as "Muslim terrorists, Islamic Jihadists, Islamic extremists, or something of the sort; and the negative media coverage is historically associated with Islam, Muhammad, and the Quran. This continues to taint and misrepresent the true picture of Islam, Muhammad, and the Quran. Not surprisingly, when "acts of terror" are committed by persons not calling themselves Muslims, media usually refers to such individuals simply as "perpetrators of violence"; hence, obvious bias.

4. Judge the person by the standard, and not the standard by the person. Anyone who says they're a Muslim, is the subject; the Quran and the excellent example of Muhammad is the standard. Neither the Quran or Muhammad condones terrorism.

5. By this same logic, we are not to put all who call themselves Christians and Jews under the same umbrella. Therefore, each Christian should be held by the standard and example of Jesus. Likewise, each person who calls themselves a Jew should be held by the standard and exemplary model of Moses. This sober minded approach helps avoid stereotyping and compels us to judge each

person by the standard, and not the standard by the person.

Chapter 4

Prayer

1. The Quran and the New Testament clearly demonstrate that Jesus and Muhammad regularly prayed to G-d, The Creator Supreme, for guidance, strength, and direction. Prayer, also referred to as Salat in Arabic, is that exclusive time when a person sets aside all other affairs to reach out and call to G-d with exclusive devotion and sincere humility. The fact that Jesus and Muhammad both prayed to The Lord our G-d, who is One G-d, is in and of itself, one of the many examples of their shared similarities.

2. This has commonly been referred to as "The Lord's Prayer." However, the author considers this title "oxymoron", for we all know that THE LORD does not pray, but we in fact pray to THE LORD! It should therefore not be referred to as "The Lord's Prayer" but rather, "Our prayer unto The Lord".

3. This prayer just so happens to be the first chapter of the Quran, called "Al Faatiha" (The Opening). In resemblance to the prayer taught by Jesus, it is comprised of seven verses. Not surprisingly, there is a noted similarity in the arrangement, tempo, and progression of supplication.

Chapter 5

Judging Other People

1. Both Jesus and Muhammad taught against "fault finding" and the habit of judging other people, without first making sure that we ourselves are acceptable and pleasing to G-d. The propensities of human behavior are such that, we are quick to judge another person, but we are not so quick or attentive to judging and evaluating ourselves. Quite the opposite, we often find a way to ignore our own faults and/or make ourselves comfortable with our shortcomings, while being "quick" to criticize and judge another person. Jesus and Muhammad both addressed this in their teaching.

Chapter 6

True Righteousness versus Superficial Gestures

1. Jesus is critically addressing the difference between doing the will of G-d, versus a superficial and pretentious allegiance to him by lip profession. He clearly denounces the idea that allegiance to him is based upon acts or gestures done merely for outward show and in his name. Jesus specifically puts the emphasis on "doing the will of

G-d" as the focus, and not a superficial and ostentatious show of allegiance to him.

2. As Jesus taught his people, Muhammad is also teaching that true righteousness in the sight of G-d, is not from mere rituals and superficial gestures, but from actually doing the will of G-d in such way that helps others.

3. In this verse, righteousness is defined by first stating that it is not based on religious rituals and gestures that give the outer appearance of devotion and worship. In this case, it was the act of facing East or West as a direction of Salat (prayer). This ritual and custom may be likened to similar customs in Judaism and Christianity regarding prayer.

4. Religious rituals and customs, albeit sacred in motive, are but signs and indicators pointing to the real actions and deeds of righteousness that benefit our community and society at large.

5. The moral logic here is that G-d has made the subject of "freeing the slaves" an issue of concern for those who claim to believe in Him. As we naturally cherish freedom and liberty for ourselves, we should desire and earnestly work towards the freedom and liberty of those who are slaves. Our moral concern should be such that, it is not pleasing to G-d that someone should be a slave for anyone, and our upright duty is to do whatever we can to help free that person from such a state, so that they can enjoy freedom and liberty as ourselves. Also, the term "slave" is not to be confused with "indentured servants." Indentured servants were typically people who agreed to work for a certain time in exchange for something else.

Slaves on the other hand, are people forced into work, subjection, bondage, and having no rights.

Chapter 7

Only G-d Is Holy and Perfectly Perfect

1. A common perception people have of Jesus is that he was holy and "perfectly perfect", and yet although he was born from his virgin mother Mary by the will of G-d, he clearly states that none but G-d is to be considered "good". "Good" in this verse and context is understood to mean perfectly perfect, holy, and without any potential for flaw. Jesus, among other noble things, represents what should be in all of us, that is, having honorable and perfect motives and intentions!

2. The meaning here is essentially the same expression Jesus said. When Jesus said that "no one is good but G-d alone, this is the same as Muhammad saying, "I am but a man like you". The moral logic of this message is two-fold; (1) only G-d is Holy and Perfectly Perfect in every sense of human contemplation, He is All-Knowing and has no need what so ever for anything, and is incapable of making a mistake or any error, (2) I (Muhammad) on the other hand, am a man just like you, having the same possibilities for honor, excellence, and a sense of perfection, but also a man just like you, having the same vulnerabilities that can lead to error and fault; I have however, committed and submitted my whole self to do the will of G-d in everything humanly possible, whatever "goodness" you see In me, is only because I serve He that is All Good.

3. In several instances noted in the New Testament, Jesus departed from his disciples to go and pray in solitude. The fact that he wanted or "felt the need" to pray to G-d, clearly demonstrates that he too needed consolation, confirmation, re-charge, and inspiration, like any other human person. Review Luke 6:12, Luke 5:16, Mathew 26:36, Mark 1:35, and Matthew 14:23 for reference.

Chapter 8

There Is But One G-d, Be Kind, Have Love for Your Fellow Man

1. During my military career, I had numerous conversations with Navy and Marine Corps personnel who were amazed to learn some of the resemblances and similarities in the teaching of Jesus and Muhammad. This helped the process of finding valuable commonalities that served as a bridge for positive exchange and productive communication.

2. Interestingly, both Jesus and Muhammad first establish the foundational principle that only G-d deserves worship. Then, they both immediately make a quick transition and focus the attention on how we are to regard and treat our fellow-man as ourselves.

3. The point emphasized here is that there is but One G-d, and that He is One and alone, having no associates or partners. This is the same exact idea corroborated by Muhammad in the reference verse from the Quran.

4. A comparison is presented here between the merit of demonstrating our love for G-d by way of loving our neighbor as we love ourselves, to all whole burnt offerings and sacrifices. Typically burnt offerings (as described in the Old Testament) was a way for an individual to make atonement for sins, and sacrifices were made to indicate one's love for G-d. Jesus is showing here that to love G-d with all your heart, soul, mind, and strength, and to love your neighbor as you love yourself, is much more because it impacts society and helps to improve humanity. This is not to underscore or cast any demerit on the previous customs. The teaching of Jesus aimed at progressing religious understanding and educating the faithful to see that our sacrifices are more productive when they benefit society.

5. If we are not in the mind set and moral disposition of having love for our parents that we do know, who cherished and sacrificed, provided for us, and raised us as children, how can we have love for our neighbor and fellow-man who we are not familiar with.

Chapter 9

Jesus and Muhammad's Parable On Wealth

1. Interestingly, we have two parables taught by Jesus and Muhammad concerning wealth and material possessions. It becomes apparent from the reading, the

parable from the Quran taught by Muhammad captures the same moral as that of the parable taught by Jesus, and even further expounds on the subject, once again, showing consistency and affirmation.

2. This is an often-taught parable in Christian sermons, emphasizing the need for the individual to be "rich with G-d", and not to be obsessed with riches of the world and material affluence. We become "rich with G-d" by first being mindful that all blessings of wealth and material affluence comes from G-d as a gift, but also as a test. We are to be grateful to G-d and give thanks to Him. We are supposed to be charitable and regardful of the needs of family and our extended neighbor. Man tends to become self-centered and pre-occupied with wealth acquisition, and not human service.

3. This state of mind identified in the parable from the Quran is essentially the same state of mind as that addressed in the parable taught by Jesus. In this state of mind, we think that because we have come into wealth and material affluence, we therefore own the keys to tomorrow's fate of happiness and success. Some people become so obsessed with their wealth and material affluence that they lose sight and think it will be ever-lasting (self-delusional). In this parable, the man had not only become self-delusional, but he also became boastful and filled with conceit.

4. The parable taught by Muhammad from the Quran included another person. This other person represents the model of how we should be. He represents the humble remembrance of G-d and that long before your acquisition of wealth, long before you got in that

favorable situation, you were merely a portion of dust (earth), then a sperm drop, and then over time you evolved into the person you are today. During our stages of growth and development from an infant, to a young child, to a young adult, and on to full maturation, we were completely dependent upon parents and extended family for support and assistance.

5. By way of parables, here is another example of similar values taught by Muhammad, that were also taught by Jesus.

Chapter 10

Jesus And Muhammad Taught Beatitudes On The Mountain

1. The subject matter of the hadiths are quite diverse and comprehensive, covering a wide range of subjects and matters of concern. It is commonly understood that, as Muhammad was being inspired and educated by the revelation of the Quran, his own personal ideas and views were being meticulously shaped and carefully refined by the wisdom of the Quran. There are, however, some hadiths referred to as "hadith Qudsi", also referred to as "sacred hadith", that are distinguished from the other hadith. It is commonly understood among Muslim scholars and the learned, that in the sacred hadith (hadith Qudsi), the words spoken by Muhammad are attributed to direct inspiration from Allah (G-d). The source of origin for all

other hadiths therefore, are understood to originate from Muhammad himself.

2. Whether we are examining the associative and related aspects of 2 similar gases such as Helium and Argon or showing the relatedness and resemblance of Jesus and Muhammad's teaching, the point is that various branches of knowledge illustrate shared properties. As for Jesus and Muhammad, the noted resemblance is highly noble.

3. A review of the principles and values presented in the two sermons of Jesus and Muhammad show a remarkable degree of like-mindedness and moral outlook.

4. In a similar fashion, psychology is a study of individual behavior, while sociology is a study of societal behavior. Each having relational significance to the other.

Chapter 11

The Proof Is In The Pudding

1. The scriptures of the Torah, Bible, and the Quran, show a natural progression of societal expansion, along with increasing issues and concerns requiring specific address. All the prophets and messengers of G-d taught essential and specific truths that paved the way for the one who would come after the prior one that was sent.

2. Since it was Muhammad that came after Jesus, it makes sense when Jesus said there were many things he would like to have said, but that "The Comforter" would

cover those things. The issue of racism and the treatment of women are two major issues he was alluding to.

3. When Muhammad uttered these words, there had already been a long trend of low estimation and disregard for women, to include not being considered as equal to men in status, and they being viewed merely as sex objects. Despite women being the mothers who bare children, raising them in the home; this role was considered menial and of low status.

4. To hunger and thirst after righteousness as described by Jesus, is similar in concept to the mentioning of "Taqwa" in the Quran. Hunger and thirst pertain to physical appetites. When you hunger for food and thirst for water, you are "driven" by the appetite to have it quenched and satisfied. Jesus uses hunger and thirst to indicate how eager and enthusiastic we are to be in seeking righteousness. The term "Taqwa" is used in the Quran to indicate a "fear of displeasing G-d". The fear of displeasing G-d makes you more conscious and accountable for your words and actions, which in turn makes you eager and enthusiastic about being right with G-d.

5. The issue of race and ethnic inferiority – superiority complex is addressed by Muhammad. Although the idea of love for your neighbor and fellow-man had already been addressed by Jesus, the human society eventually needed more specific address and direct language to speak to this specific issue. Muhammad clearly denounces the idea of race or ethnic superiority, and states that the only one who is more favored or superior is the one who has more

"Taqwa" (reverence and fear of displeasing G-d); which as previously described, is essentially the same as the idea of hungering and thirsting after righteousness as taught by Jesus.

6. Jesus had previously stated that everyone who says to him, "Lord, Lord, will not enter the kingdom of heaven (Matthew 7:21) of the New Testament, but that only the one who does the will of G-d. This is also why he said, "You are the salt of the earth, but what good is salt if it has lost its savor?" By inference then, Jesus knew that some who claim to be his followers would fall short. By the same token, Muhammad also knew that some who claimed to follow him would also fall short. This is the reason why in his farewell address on the mountain, Muhammad said, "It maybe that the last ones may understand my words better than those who are present and listening now". By inference, he too knew the probability of some of his own followers also falling short and drifting away from his message and example.

Chapter 12

Jesus And Muhammad: Prophets Of The One G-d

1. As two prophets sent by G-d, Jesus and Muhammad had some experiences that were obviously similar, especially in terms of how people responded to their message. There were however, unique differences in certain

audience settings between the two. Jesus was often speaking in villages and towns among what was considered the "common folk", but he was also often among the Pharisees, Saducees, Doctors of Law, and priests in the temples. Muhammad on the other hand, was often teaching among the common folk of Mecca and Medina, but also had dialogue amongst Jews, especially in Medina. Difference of audience settings and immediate issues of concern would naturally determine the focus of attention.

2. The people of Jesus era were expecting a different type of leader to come. His style of teaching, with the use of parables, metaphors, and by not always quoting from the Law of Moses, made some of the religious leadership weary and very cautious. So he told them, "I have not come to destroy the Law or the prophets, but to fulfill".

3. The idea of Jesus preaching deliverance to the captives and setting at liberty those that are bruised, is equivalent and compatible with the ransoming of slaves as taught by Muhammad from the Quran.

Chapter 13

Jesus And Muhammad Advocated Active Participation

1. We are living in a time that truly challenges our faith and claimed beliefs in a major way. An example we all are quite familiar with is the issue of racism and inferiority - superiority complexes based on ethnicity, that continue to reap havoc in our society. If there was ever a time for religious leadership to make a "joyful noise unto the Lord", that time would be now. Many religious leaders and general membership however, have lost their "savor" as Jesus mentioned, when instructing to his followers to be as "salt for the earth" and "light for the world". Many religious leaders and general membership are more afraid to take a stand and at a minimum, boldly speak out against the climate of racism in our country and advocate what is right.

2. The message from the Quran that Muhammad taught is essentially saying the same thing Jesus taught. As such, Jesus and Muhammad both taught that true believers in G-d have the awesome responsibility of being the "check-and-balance" for society, and that they must constantly represent the voice of truth, fairness, and equality. The true believer in G-d cannot claim to be filled with the spirit of G-d, claim to be a follower of Jesus or Muhammad, and yet act oblivious to the societal injustices and climate of racism right in their midst. This should be the moral position for every church, synagogue, and mosque throughout our society. To simply put on a "cosmetic display" of devotion at the house of worship on Sunday, Friday, Saturday, or any other day considered its Sabbath, and to not be serving as "salt of the earth" and

"light for the world" in the broader community and world at large, at least by speaking out against the wrong and advocating what is right; is a poor representation for anyone claiming to be followers of Jesus or Muhammad.

Chapter 14

JESUS PROMISED THE COMING OF THE COMFORTER, MUHAMMAD IS THE COMFORTER PROMISED BY JESUS

1. https://en.wikipedia.org/wiki/Language_of_Jesus

2. https://en.wikipedia.org/wiki/Biblical_Aramaic

3. www.thearamaicscriptures.com/1st-john.html

4. These 6 reference verses indicate and prove that the Holy Spirit was already present, therefore there was no need to predict about the Holy Spirit coming, it was already there.

5. Per the New Testament, it was common for Jesus to use parables and metaphors when teaching to various audiences, (see Luke 8:10 and Matthew 13:10). Subsequently, it is not surprising that many people misunderstood the true meanings of certain terms and concepts Jesus was trying to convey. (see Matthew 13: 1 – 23) It is evident from this reading that many would hear but not understand, and many would see but not truly perceive, as noted in Isaiah 6:9 of the Old Testament.

Chapter 15

Muhammad: A Brief Sketch

1. The early life of Muhammad was obviously impacted by the loss of his father, mother, and grandfather, at an early age.

2. Despite having been orphaned by age 6, historians report that Muhammad's personal development and likeability among the people of Mecca, gave him much favor and estimation among the adults who encountered him.

3. Historians report that Muhammad was often called by 2 distinct nick-names, El-Amin (The Trustworthy) and El Sadeeq (The Honest and Truthful), even as a young adult. Jesus referred to The Comforter as "The Spirit of Truth". There is an obvious correlation between the nick-names given to Muhammad and the nick-name Jesus gave to The Comforter. It is highly unlikely that this is by mere chance or random incident. The very words "Spirit of Truth" is consistent with the description, "The Trustworthy" and "The Honest and Truthful".

4. Long before any encounters with the angel Gabriel for receiving revelations of the Quran, Muhammad had already showed strong disfavor and disagreement with the uncivil and immoral practices of "Jahiliyyah" Mecca. Not surprisingly, this is a reason why historians note that Muhammad would often seek solitude away from Mecca. It is noted that he would often go to a cave in the mountains called Hira, to temporarily withdraw himself from the chaos, idolatry, and moral decadence that had engulfed Mecca.

5. The low estimation and inferior status of women has been ubiquitous throughout history in every culture.

6. It is well documented that female infanticide was prevalent in other parts of the world, however, it had become rampant and such an ignorant and immoral practice in Arabia. It is recorded that such practice was typically done out of either fear of disgrace, or fear of poverty. Also, male chauvinism was truly at its height, so much so, that the news of a female birth often brought on a sense of weakness and shame among men in the tribes that occupied Arabia. The birth of sons was favored; the birth of daughters was not.

7. The fulfillment of prophecy refers to the prophecy of Jesus foretelling the coming of "The Comforter". When referring to "The Comforter" Jesus said, "he will not speak from his own accord, but will speak what he hears". (New Testament John 16: 7 – 14)

8. Numerous historians report that long before Muhammad began to receive revelations from G-d by way of the angel Gabriel, he had acquired 2 nicknames that people commonly referred to him as, (1) "El-Amin" which means The Trustworthy, and (2) "El Sadeeq", which means The Honest and Truthful. The author contends that these acquired nicknames and the fact that Jesus refers to "The Comforter" as "The Spirit of Truth", is not a coincidence. The dots are there to be connected.

9. The narrated appearance of the angel Gabriel to Muhammad, is consistent with the narrated appearance of Gabriel to Daniel, Zachariah, and Mary, the mother of

Jesus, Per the New Testament. In all cases, Gabriel is the angel that brings pertinent news and specific messages from G-d. Undoubtedly, G-d has communicated to His prophets and messengers by various mediums; Gabriel however, is specifically the angel of news and revelation.

10. Prior to Muhammad receiving revelations of the Quran and him beginning to preach openly in Mecca, he was perceived as a pleasant complement, welcomed by all who encountered him. The moment he began to preach openly, denouncing the pagan idols as objects to be worshipped, denouncing the pagan customs such as the killing of female infants, denouncing the unfair treatment of women, advocating the liberation of slaves; he immediately became the object of scorn and rejection from the people of Mecca, especially the leaders of the tribes. Interestingly, as Waraqah informed Muhammad that a prophet was always without honor in his own country, Jesus also said. "a prophet is not without honor, but in his own country, and among his own kin, and in his own house". (New Testament, Luke 4:24 and Mark 6:4 – 6)

11. The first and perhaps most arduous "sin" Muhammad began to rebuke was the sin of worshipping idols and any graven image as G-d. He denounced the idea of ascribing divinity to any person, object, or any image as G-d, or having any association with G-d. The message from the Quran that Muhammad taught was that, The Creator Supreme cannot be seen with the naked eye, because He is not of material substance or created matter, rather, He is The Creator of all created matter, but He is not material and cannot be represented by any physical or material form. He taught that G-d is One and alone, and

that He does not share His rule, and that everyone is subject to G-d as a servant. The message of the Quran that Muhammad taught not only rebuked the sins of idolatry and pagan worship that was common in Mecca, but he also rebuked the sin of ascribing divine like attributes to others, thus considering them equal to G-d.

12. In rebuking the idea of righteousness, the teachings of Muhammad from the Quran transitions from abstract beliefs into practical actions and deeds that are intended to benefit people in society. This was necessary because for many, the idea of righteousness had come to be measured by such things as ceremonial burnt offerings and animal sacrifices, and other acts often displayed for ostentatious show. In reproving righteousness, the teaching of Muhammad from the Quran was designed to re-educate man that righteousness to G-d is measured by our actions and deeds that assist and benefit society.

13. The idea of "reproving judgement" obviously pertains to how people co-exist with one another in the social context. Jesus already knew that "The Comforter" would have to address critical social issues relating to how people judged and viewed each other in the global context, and how they should be able to get along. Jesus had already laid foundational principles of this in his Sermon on the Mount, referred to as "The Beatitudes". Not surprisingly, Muhammad addressed 2 of the perhaps most critical issues affecting social justice and fairness, and that is, (1) the issue of race and ethnic inferiority - superiority complexes and (2) the issue of regard for fair and equitable treatment of women.

Chapter 16

The Quran: The Message Heard By Muhammad

1. Jesus readily gives honor and praise to G-d as The One who granted him his abilities. In other words, his abilities and powers were not innate or automatic, but rather, they were bestowed upon him from G-d. In John 5:30 of the New Testament, Jesus says, "I can do nothing on my own, as I hear, I judge, and my judgement is just, because I seek not my own will, but the will of Him who sent me".

2. Historians and religious scholars alike convey that Muhammad was an uneducated man of Mecca. It is therefore only plausible that the descriptions of certain scientific phenomenon conveyed in the Quran could only be from G-d, The All-Knowing Creator.

Chapter 17

Authenticity Of The Quran

1. In this verse from the Quran, the Arabic word "alaq" is of utmost significance. This Arabic word "alaq" has in its meanings, "a leech-like germ cell clinging and attached". We know today that during fertilization, the early life form(egg) travels down the fallopian tube to the uterus. We also know today that once it is in the uterus, it immediately starts to "implant itself" into the wall of the

uterus. Once successfully implanted, it is thereafter referred to as an embryo. The question naturally follows; how could Muhammad have known this process and that early life is formed by a fertilized egg successfully implanted and becoming "attached and fastened" to the uterus; thus, the connotative meaning of "alaq"?

2. In this verse, man is reminded that he has been created from dust (Turrab), then from sperm (Nuutfatin), then out of a germ cell attached in the uterus, then out of a morsel of flesh, partly formed and partly unformed (fetus). The only way for Muhammad to have known this developmental process and proclaim this highly complexed information, was for it to have been conveyed by G-d, The One who designed this process. This exact knowledge was not known at the time. What did exist, was unfounded theory and hypothesis.

3. The Arabic word "Amshaj" is referring to the sperm of the male and ovum of the female, which join during fertilization to form the embryo. Interestingly there is the mentioning of the two senses, hearing and seeing. We know today, that sound is present at around 20 weeks and eye movement at even 14 weeks. The fact that hearing is mentioned first, then seeing, is consistent with what we know today of fetal development. Medical sources report that hearing occurs as early as 20 weeks. The fact of it mentioned here indicates this could only have been conveyed to Muhammad from G-d, the Creator and Guardian-Evolver of the human life process.

4. The three veils of darkness has several implications, one of which refers to the biological-physiological stages (transitions) of pregnancy. We know today that the stages of pregnancy are divided into 3 transitions because of the distinct and profound developmental changes (at weeks 1 – 12, weeks 13 – 28, and weeks 29 -40). The obvious question is; how could Muhammad have known this exact information about the three stages (transitions) at that time, when such medical confirmation was not known until hundreds of years later? The only rational explanation is that this knowledge was revealed by The Creator, The One who created the stages of human development.

5. *On Animal Generation*, was a major work of William Harvey in 1651, in which the foundation of contemporary embryology was detailed. His work proved false the previous held ideas known as "spontaneous generation", and as well, it disproved the theory held by Aristotle, of semen and blood. Again, the question to ask is, how could Muhammad, who by all accounts was an unschooled, uneducated man, how could he have known this highly complexed information, and intelligently present it in a book, when such information was not available?

The only plausible explanation that could be is, that this information was conveyed to him by G-d, The Creator Supreme, The One who designed the stages of human development.

Chapter 18

The Seven Layers of Sky and Earth

1. https://evidencesofcreation.wordpress.com/2012/04/24/the-layers-of-the-atmosphere/.

2. https://prezi.com/v2ev8od3hyjy/the-7-layers-of-the-earth/.

Chapter 19

How Did Muhammad Know The Universe Was Expanding?

1. Early scientific thinkers and philosophers such as Aristotle and Ptolemy conceived the universe as being geocentric, stressing that the universe was "unchanged and static". This view was also believed by such minds as Isaac Newton and even Albert Einstein.

2. Albert Einstein was compelled to abandon his theory of an "unchanging and static universe" when, in 1929, Edwin Hubble proved and confirmed that our universe was indeed steadily and continuously expanding. The fact of

the matter is, this had already been revealed to Muhammad in the Quran hundreds of years earlier. Surprisingly, Muhammad did not have a highly complexed telescope as did Edwin Hubble. Muhammad had revelation from G-d, the Lord of all worlds and systems of knowledge.

Chapter 20

The Barrier between Fresh Water and Salt Water in the seas

1. In his book entitled "Principles of Oceanography", pages 92 -93, Oceanographer Richard A. Davis expounds on this amazing phenomenon whereby salt water and fresh water are partitioned / separated, as stated in the Quran. His book detailing this unique occurrence, was published in 1977. The message of the Quran, which had already established this distinct feature, was revealed to Muhammad over 1400 years ago. Muhammad of course, was not an Oceanographer, Marine Biologist, Surveyor, or one tutored in any field of scientific inquiry. For Muhammad to assert this unique fact about the barrier /partition between fresh water and salt water over 1400 years ago, without having the ability to navigate through the depths of the water as the Challenger expedition of 1872-76, it would have to mean that this precise information was conveyed to him by "The One" who made fresh water and salt water, The All-Knowing Creator.

Chapter 21

Defeat and Victory of the Roman Empire

1. The verse in the Quran (chapter 30 verses 2 -4) that predicted the time frame at which the Romans would be victorious even after their defeat, is expressed in Arabic as *"biddi sineen"*, which is often translated and understood to mean a small number, a range between 3 and 9 years.

2. https://en.wikipedia.org/wiki/Battle_of_Nineveh(627)

Chapter 22

Jesus and Muhammad Practiced Fasting

1. This verse from the Quran states that fasting was "prescribed" for Muhammad and his followers, just as fasting was "prescribed" for many before him (Jesus, Moses, Abraham, etc.). In other words, this was not a new or arbitrary practice. The observance of fasting to draw closer to G-d, is well documented throughout the Biblical scriptures.

Chapter 23

Jesus and Muhammad Taught Principles of Interfaith

1. Mark 6:3 and Matthew 13: 55-56 indicate that Jesus had 4 brothers; James, Joses or Joseph, Jude, and Simon.

2. Per the New Testament, Jesus often used parables and metaphorical examples to convey an idea. Here he states, "whoever does the will of G-d, is my brother". By inference, Jesus is giving the same honor and recognition we would naturally have for our biological mother, brother, or sister, to who so ever does the will of G-d. This is the central idea of Interfaith.

3. The Sabians were a religious community that were present in Arabia before Muhammad. It is reported their beliefs and practices had some resemblance to Judaism, Christianity, and even Zoroastrianism. It has also been reported that they read from the "Zaboor", also known as the Psalms of David. In short, because of their monotheistic orientation, they are extended equal consideration and honorable mention along with Muslims, Christians, and Jews.

4. "Lita Aarafu", is the Arabic expression of the Quran which conveys the meaning of becoming acquainted with, becoming familiar with, getting to know each other, so

that you can live with respect and consideration amongst each other; and not with strife and contempt for each other. The idea here is that G-d created us all, and in His Wisdom and Perfect Plan, He intended for there to be diversity of race, culture, language, etc. He intended for us all to have enough "Common Sense" to recognize our shared commonalities. Therefore, the one who is most excellent is neither the black or the white, nor the Arab or the non-Arab, nor is it the one who calls themselves Muslim, Christian, Jew, or any other religious name; the one who is most excellent in the sight of G-d is the one who is most G-d fearing and mindful of their duty to Him, the one who is most eager to do His Will and strive for excellence. This is the teaching of Muhammad from the Quran, and it is equivalent to the teaching of Jesus where he said, "Blessed are those who hunger and thirst after righteousness".

BIBLIOGRAPHY

Ali, Abdullah Yusuf. 1997. *The Meaning of The Holy Quran*. Amana Publications. 1997

Al-Mubarakpuri, Safi-ur-Rahman. 1979. *The Sealed Nectar*. Biography of the Noble Prophet. DARUSSALAM. 1979

Armstrong, Karen. 2007. *Muhammad, A Prophet For Our Time*. HarperCollins Publishers. 2007

Bible. King James Version. http://biblehub.com/

Bible. New American Standard Bible. http://biblehub.com

Borg, Marcus. J. 1991. *Jesus, A New Vision*. Spirit, Culture, and The Life of Discipleship. HarperSanFrancisco. A Division of HarperCollinsPublishers. 1991

Fillmore, Charles. 2005. *Metaphysical Bible Dictionary*. Charles Fillmore Reference Library Series. 1995

Griffith, Sidney. H. 2010. *The Church in the Shadow of the Mosque*. Christians and Muslims in the World of Islam. Princeton University Press. 2010

Hart, Michael. H. 1992. *The 100*. A Ranking Of The Most Influential Persons In History. Citadel Press. Kensington Publishing Corp. 1992

Hayal, Muhammad Husayn. 1993. *The Life of Muhammad.* American Trust Publications. 1993

Maududi, Sayyid Abul Ala. 1972. *Tafhim al-Quran - The Meaning of the Quran.* http://www.englishtafsir.com/Quran/30/index.html. Accessed January 9, 2018

Mohammed, W. Deen.2015. *Mohammad The Prophet.* The Perfect Man - The Complete Man. WDM Publications LLC. 2015

Omar, Abdul Mannan. 2010. *Dictionary of The Holy Quran.* Arabic-English. NOOR Foundation - International Inc. 2010

Reeves, John, ed. *Bible and Quran; Essays in Scriptual Intertexuality.* Symposium Series, no. 24. Atlanta: Society of Biblical Literature, 2003

Rogerson, Barnaby. 2003. *The Prophet Muhammad.* A Biography. ABACUS. 2003

Shaheed, Ronald B. 2014. *The Promised Human Destiny.* Reflections of W. Deen Mohammed. Published by Imam Ronald B Shaheed. 2014

Siljander, Mark D. 2008. *A Deadly Misunderstanding.* A Congressman's Quest To Bridge The Muslim - Christian Divide. HaperOne, An Imprint of HarperCollinsPublishers. 2008

Sirry, Mun'im A. "Early Muslim-Christian Dialogue: A Closer Look at Major Themes of the Theological

Encounter." *Islam and Christian-Muslim Relations* 16 (2005): 361-76

Sweetman, James W. *Islam and Christian Theology: A Study of the Interpretation of Theological Ideas in the two Religions.* 2 vols. In 4. London. Lutterworth Press, 1954-67

INDEX

A

Abdullah (Muhammad's father), 105
Abraham, 64, 205
Ai lun, Ts`, 176
Alaq, 114, 129, 200 - 201
Al Fatiha, 24, 147
Amshaj, 130, 201
Arab, 61, 65, 68, 71, 109 – 110, 158, 207
Arabic, 27, 41, 131, 157, 182, 200 – 201, 205 - 206
Aramaic, 27, 90 – 92, 195

B

Beatitudes, 18, 58 – 59, 174, 189, 199, 211, 214
Bell. Alexander Graham, 176
Bible, 9, 15, 17 – 18, 36, 113, 115, 146, 190
Biddi sineen, 205
Black, 61, 65, 68, 71, 158, 207

C

Charity, 31, 33, 35, 65, 68, 78, 118
Christianity, 9, 22, 73, 89, 96, 142, 159, 168, 184, 206
Christians, 22, 37, 67, 73, 89, 92, 109, 145, 151, 153 – 155, 159, 161 – 162, 164, 166, 168, 181, 206
Comforter (The), 89, 90 – 93, 95 – 105, 114, 116 – 117, 119 – 122, 181, 190, 195 – 197, 199
Copernicus, Nicholaus, 176

D

David (prophet), 206
Day of Judgement, 24, 33
Drew, Dr. Charles, 176
Dynamic Duo, 175 - 177

E

Edison, Thomas, 176
Einstein, Albert, 6, 136 – 137, 176, 203
El-Amin (The Trustworthy), 106 – 108, 111, 121, 196 - 197
El-Sadeeq (The Truthful, The Honest), 106 – 108, 111, 121, 196 - 197
Equality, 70 – 71, 79 – 80, 102 – 103, 115, 119 – 120, 151, 158, 194
Ethnic, 14, 64, 67, 70 – 73, 80, 102 – 103, 116, 119 – 120, 151, 157 – 158, 191, 194, 199

F

Freedom, 34 – 35, 109, 184

G

Galilei, Galileo, 176
God, 11, 43 – 44, 65, 94, 110, 178
Gutenberg, Johann, 176

H

Hadith (reported sayings of Muhammad), 18, 60, 63, 177, 189 - 190
Harvey, William, 132, 176, 202
Hajj, 60 – 61, 63 – 65, 68
Hira (cave), 111 – 112, 128, 145, 196
Holy Spirit, 41, 92 – 100, 103, 122, 195
Hubble, Edwin, 136 – 137, 176, 203 - 204

I

Idols, 109, 112, 118, 198
Interfaith, 149, 151 – 152, 154, 158, 164, 166 – 167, 169 – 170, 206
Islam, 9, 21, 73, 89, 159, 168, 178, 181, 208
Israel, 43, 91, 94, 101, 171 - 172

J

Jahiliyyah (Period of Ignorance) 108, 110, 117, 146, 196
Jerusalem, 58, 63, 90, 94, 163
Jews, 22, 67, 89, 101, 109, 154 ‑ 155, 159, 161 ‑ 162, 164, 166, 168, 181, 193, 206
John, (The Baptist), 95
Judaism, 9, 22, 159, 168, 184, 206
Judging (others), 29 ‑ 30, 73, 193

K

Kepler, Johannes, 176
Khadijah, 107 ‑ 108, 110, 114
Kingdom of Heaven, 31 ‑ 32, 35, 58 ‑ 59, 64, 67 ‑ 68, 75, 192

L

Leeuwenhoek, Antonie Van, 176
Lord's prayer, 147, 182
Love (your neighbor), 44, 47 ‑ 48, 187
Luke (New Testament), 17, 37 ‑ 38, 41, 51, 70, 76, 91, 94 ‑ 95, 113, 119, 163, 186, 195, 198

M

Mark (New Testament), 43, 46, 70, 119, 150, 152, 157, 159, 164 ‑ 168, 170, 186, 198, 206
Mary (mother of Jesus), 94 ‑ 95, 113 ‑ 115, 150, 167, 185, 197
Matthew (New Testament), 11, 15, 23, 26 ‑ 27, 29, 31, 35, 58, 63, 70, 75, 82, 91, 94, 101, 119, 145 ‑ 146, 186, 192, 195, 206
Mecca, 60, 63, 105 ‑ 112, 115 ‑ 117, 121, 127, 142, 145 ‑ 146, 193, 196, 198 ‑ 200
Medina, 193
Miracles, 39 ‑ 40, 94, 124 ‑ 125
Moses, 20, 22, 75 ‑ 76, 180 ‑ 181, 193, 205

N

Nazareth, 76, 90
Newton, Isaac, 176, 203
Nineveh, The Battle of, 143, 205

O

Oppression, 35, 81

P

Pagan, 107, 109 – 111, 142, 145, 198 – 199
Paraclete, 92
Peshitta (Aramaic New Testament), 92
Prayer, 11, 16, 23 – 27, 29, 31, 33, 35, 40 – 41, 61, 64 – 65, 68, 78, 118, 147, 182, 184

Q

Quran, 9, 15 – 16, 18, 20 – 21, 24, 26, 29 – 36, 38 – 39, 41 – 43, 45 – 52, 54 – 56, 58, 60, 62, 74, 78, 80, 85 – 88, 104 – 105, 116, 118, 121, 123 – 144, 146, 149, 151 – 158, 160 – 161, 165 – 166, 168, 170, 173 – 176, 180 – 182, 187 - 191

R

Racism, 70 – 71, 80, 102 – 103, 119 – 120, 169, 191, 194
Ramadan, 61, 65, 68, 111

S

Satan, 61
Sermon on the Mount (Beatitudes), 18, 58 – 59, 174, 199
Simeon, 94 - 95
Slavery, 35, 70, 79

T

Taqwa, 191 - 192

Terrorist, 21, 181
Trinity, 96

U
Universe (expanding), 136 - 137, 144, 203

V
Violence, (acts of), 181

W
Waraqah, 114 - 115, 198
Wisdom, 39 - 40, 97, 124, 130, 157, 170, 189, 207

Z
Zachariah, 113 - 115, 197